Sex:
The Catholic Experience

Sex:
The Catholic
Experience

by Andrew Greeley

ACKNOWLEDGMENTS

Portions of the material in this book have previously appeared in different form in *America* magazine.

Cover Design: Davidson Design
Interior Design: Pamela Glick
Art Direction: Karen McDonald

Send all inquiries to:
Tabor Publishing
200 East Bethany Drive
Allen, Texas 75002-3804

Printed in the United States of America

ISBN 0-88347-285-6

1 2 3 4 5 6   98 97 96 95 94

Contents

NOTE: Since this book is intended for the general reader, I have kept tables and charts at a minimum because both tend to scare off those who think that column of numbers or lines and bars on a page are somehow obscure. They have also been positioned at the end of the chapters, so a reader who does not like charts (which are nothing more than pictures to illustrate an argument in the text) may safely ignore them all. However, there is no way that numbers, either percentages or correlation coefficients, can be omitted from the text and the book remain an exercise in empirical sociology.

Social scientists who want more rather than less numbers can write me NORC, The University of Chicago, 60637.

Marriage as the Great Sacrament.
  St. Paul's metaphor in Ephesians 5:22–33

*"All of us have access to a genuine spiritual
experience which is uniquely our own. The
point about power is not so much that it inhibits
such an experience in some people as that it
controls how this is valued or even recognized
for what it is."*
  Philip Sheldrake in **Spirituality and History**

*"Christian spouses and parents can and should
offer their unique and irreplaceable contribution
to the elaboration of an authentic evangelical
discernment in the various situations and cultures
in which men and women live their marriage
and their family life. They are qualified for the
role by their charisma or specific gift, the gift of
the sacrament of matrimony."*
  Pope John Paul II in **Familiaris Consortio**

"Love is the heartbeat of the universe."
  Alfredo Germont in Verdi's **La Traviata**

*"In no species besides humans has the purpose
of copulation become so unrelated to reproduction."*
  Jared Diamond in **The Third Chimpanzee**

Introduction

This is a book about the Catholic experience of sex. It is not based on a priori theological or spiritual doctrines, but rather on the actual sexual experiences of American Catholics as recorded in surveys.

Some will think perhaps that the title and the theme is an oxymoron: Catholics are not permitted by their Church to experience sex. Those who think that will be in for a surprise.

Some will think perhaps that it is absurd to contend that there is anything special about Catholic sexual experience. How can it be and why should it be different from the sexual experience of others—unless the sexual repression in the Church has made Catholic sex less satisfactory than the sex of other Americans? Those who think that will be in for a surprise.

Some will think perhaps that "secularization" is progressed so far in the United States that it is quite impossible that religion will correlate with different styles of sexuality. Those who think that will be in for a surprise.

Some Catholic leaders will think, sadly, that because of the changes of the last thirty years, American Catholics will have become like everyone else in their approach to sexuality and that therefore there will be nothing distinctive about their sexual ethos. Those who think that will be in for a surprise.

The Catholic experience of sex is not utterly unique. But, on the average, it is not exactly like that of other Americans either. It is somewhat different. Those who think they know what that difference is will be in for a surprise.

Thus, many readers will be in for a great deal of surprise as I was when the pieces of the picture began to fall into place—despite the fact that my theories of the sociology of religion had led me to predict the direction of the differences.

This book will not be an exhaustive study of Catholic sexuality because the data do not exist for such a study and are not likely to exist, not even when the scholars working on AIDS research in various countries are ready to release their data to other scholars—something they have been most reluctant to do in what many would see as a violation of the norms and mores of the survey research fraternity. Even when such data finally do become available, they will not permit the kind of analysis attempted in several chapters of this book because, like most American social scientists, the scholars working on the AIDS surveys do not think that religion is important—and no amount of evidence to the contrary will change their minds.[1]

The picture in this book will be partial, but it will be complete enough to suggest to all save those who have already irrevocably made up their minds on the matter that the Catholic experience of sex is somewhat different. Ideally, the Church itself should fund research in the directions indicated by this book on the sexual experiences of its lay folk. So, too, ideally the Chicago Cubs will win the World Series next year.

During the last decade and a half, I have engaged in a number of different analyses of Catholics and sex. One of the reasons is that as the one who discovered the turn away from the birth control teaching by the laity and the lower clergy (and thus earned myself permanent marginality in the institutional Church), I have had perforce to stay in touch with what is going on in Catholic sexual behavior if only to defend myself from the rage of Catholic leaders and the ridicule of Catholic "liberals."

A more important reason is that I have developed a theory of the sociology of religion which leads me to believe that St.

Paul was right when he postulated in the Epistle to the Ephesians an intimate link between human and divine love. As data came available from the Young Catholic Study and the General Social Survey at the National Opinion Research Center and the Gallup-collected data on which I based my book *Faithful Attraction* (Tor Books, 1991), I tested the theory at every opportunity. The chapters in this book are, for the most part, the results of such tests or of inquiries to which the tests led me. The various analyses were episodic in the sense that they dealt with specific questions which specific times and circumstances raised. But they were all done under the umbrella of one overarching theory. It seemed appropriate to draw them together in one book and attempt to make systematic sense of the apparently unique Catholic experience of sexuality.

The basic premise of my theory is that religion is the story[2] (of God) we tell to ourselves and to others in order to explain what our life means. The basic expectation of my theory is that religious stories will be predictive of other stories. Our relationship to the Other will be predictive of our relationships to others, both intimate and distant. Our religious stories will correlate with our familial, political, social, artistic, and common sense stories. The correlations will not be large because in social science no correlations are all that big and because other events and stories will intervene between religion and the rest of life. But if religion is to be a useful predictor variable in social research, the best way to measure it will be to measure religious stories and not doctrinal convictions or church attendance.

Religion originates in EXPERIENCES which renew hope, is encoded in our memories through pictures or SYMBOLS which recall those experiences, shared with others in STORIES (normally the others being members of a storytelling COMMUNITY) and often acted out in community RITUALS.

Religion, it is assumed by my theory, is rooted in the human capacity to hope; a capacity which Lionel Tiger has suggested may be genetic but is, in any case, ineradicable. Reinforcing this propensity to hope, and probably a consequent of it, is the human capacity to experience moments of "gratuity"; such moments (David Tracy in *Blessed Rage for Order* [Seabury, 1973], calls them "limit experiences") may be relatively minor, such as a summer day, a cold silent sheet of ice on the lake in wintertime, a touch of a friendly hand, a smile of a two-year-old; or they may be the major ecstatic experiences of the sort described by William James or any kind of intense continuum between moments of "revelation" or "gratuity" that would appear on these extremes. These moments of gratuity—they may also be called moments of "grace"—are "sacraments" (with a small s) or "revelations" (with a small r) which seem to reveal a secret design or purpose or goodness or order at work in this cosmos. In these experiences of "grace," one may find the origin both of religious heritages which developed through history and of the religious perspectives which developed the biography of an individual person.

These experiences are resonated and recounted to people as "symbols" or "images" or "pictures" which spontaneously arise in their own imaginative process to help them to articulate what they have experienced. Such "symbols" are drawn both from people's own religious tradition and from the general repertoire of powerful imagery which is at the disposal of humankind (sun, moon, light, water, fire, food, sex, etc.). Often the core of religious heritage can be found by examining what use it makes of the human symbol repertoire.

Such religious symbols resonating, representing, and articulating—still at the imaginative level and in the imaginative dimension of the personality—are in fact "stories" which purport to provide meaning both to the life of the individual person and the existence of the cosmos. These religious stories implicitly and imaginatively link the experiences of an individual's life with that Higher Order which has been experienced in moments of "gratuity" or "grace." One might add that in this approach to religion Sacraments (with a capital S) and Revelations (with a capital R) are those experiences and symbols—the exodus experience of the Hebrew people, the death and resurrection of Jesus, for example—in which a given religious tradition emphatically reaffirms, confirms, validates, and revalidates the fundamental moments of hopefulness that all humans encounter in their lives.

A religious symbol then is an articulation of an experience of hope. Such symbols are implicitly "stories" which link the stories of a life of an individual person with what the person perceives to be the larger Story of the cosmos. Such symbols not only represent for the person and give meaning for what has happened so far in his/her own story, but they also shape the development of that story since they describe the "scenery" and the "setting" with which the rest of the individual's story will unroll.

All of this activity occurs initially and primordially in the creative or the imaginative dimension of the personality. It is called by Leonard Kubie "the preconscious" and "the creative imagination," by Jacques Maritain "the creative faculty" and "agent intellect" (here Maritain would be following Aquinas and Aristotle), and by St. Paul "our spirit" (to which The Spirit speaks). Since humans are more than imaginative and poetic creatures, they very quickly reflect intellectually on, philosophize about, and then theologize about their moments of grace and then express a digested version of these theologies in credal statements and catechetical propositions. Such statements and propositions, of course, are "religious," but they are not primordially religious in the sense that the experiences of grace and the stories which produce these experiences can be said to be primordially and fundamentally religious. If one wishes to know then the religious orientation of a human personality, one must look not only to his/her catechetical propositions and credal statements but also and more importantly to his/her religious imagery and the stories implicit in such imagery. For the purpose of the present research, I am assuming that the experiences of childhood relationships are "sacramental" in that they reveal to a child something about the nature of the cosmos and the possibility of his/her own existence. I assume that these experiences of childhood affect an adult's religious imagery and that religious imagery in turn affects his/her approach to human intimacy and human love. Quite simply put, the warmer the childhood experiences have been, the warmer a person's religious imagination will be, and the warmer will be his/her own marital intimacy. No argument is made that all the religious imagery is shaped by childhood experience or that all of the quality of the warmth of the marriage is shaped by the warmth of religious imagery that a husband and wife may have. Such an expectation would be absurd because both religious imagery and marital satisfaction are complex phenomena likely to be shaped by many different aspects of a person's biological, psychological, cultural, and biographic background. I do not, in other words, expect particularly high correlations among the variables with which I will be working, but I do expect there to be real and statistically significant correlations.

If the experiences of the family of origin are revelatory, so, too, are the experiences of the family of procreation. Husbands and wives "reveal" to one another whether the "Real" is benign or malign, "warm" or "cold." When two people marry they merge their individual stories into a common story. "Your" story and "my" story become "our" story. Your religious imagery influences my religious imagery, and vice versa. Therefore, there will be a tendency for husband and wife to converge in their religious imagery in the course of the marriage. Convergence will in part be the result of their experiences of love but will also have a profound influence on the further development of their marital satisfaction. Husband and wife are a "sacrament" for one another, "grace" for one another (in the sociological if not the theological sense). Therefore, a substantial amount of the ebb and flow, the rise and decline, and rise again of the quality of their relationship will be interpretable in terms of the changing patterns of their religious imagery.

The propositions in the previous paragraph may seem reasonable enough when one reads them. Unfortunately for the empirical sociologist, it is not enough to articulate plausible and attractive ideas. One must submit such ideas to falsification or verification against empirical data. One must test the possibility that those who are more likely to think of God as a lover are also more likely to be better lovers themselves, a proposition which would seem ridiculous to the sophisticated conventional wisdom.

While I think the subjects and predicates in my theory fit together and that the sentences and paragraphs make sense, I find it hard to persuade both sociologists and theologians to listen to the theory. Both seem so determined to think of religion as doctrine and devotion that they are incapable of entertaining a possibility (which for the sociologists at any rate is part of their tradition) that the pre-rational components of religion might be much more important.

My theory of the sociology of religion owes something to each of the classic theories of the sociology of religion. With Karl Marx, I believe that religion is profoundly influenced by the social context in which believers find themselves, including the context of their own religious heritage.

With Sigmund Freud, I believe that religion is in substantial part shaped by the family of origin. My analyses will show that religious devotion is influenced by the devotion of the parents, particularly the father, and by the quality of the relationship of the parents with the self and with each other, and that relationships with parents substantially influence the narrative symbols, the religious stories with which one attempts to explain the meaning of life.

With Emile Durkheim, I believe that the experience of the collectivity in ritual behavior has an enormous impact on religious faith and is one of the primary means of passing on religious heritages.

With Bronislaw Malinowski, I believe that religion is often the binding force which holds human communities together in times of crisis.

With Max Weber, I believe that religion provides values and meaning which shape human behavior in society as well as being shaped by society.

With Taclott Parsons and Clifford Geertz, I believe that religion is essentially a meaning system.

With Georg Simmel, Rudolph Otto, and William James, I believe that religion takes its origin and its raw power from experiences—of respect, of the holy, of the transcendent.

And with Mircea Eliade, I believe that triggers for religious experience lurk everywhere—in the objects, events, and persons of everyday life which can, on certain occasions, lead to experiences in which hope is renewed.

There are two tools which have proven useful in the development and testing of my theory: the distinction between the popular tradition and the high tradition, and the comparison of the analogical and dialectical imaginations. A heritage contains many different versions of its story; it is convenient for my purposes to group them (or most of them) under the headings of the poetic and the prose traditions, or the popular and the high traditions. The former is the tradition of experience and story, the latter the tradition of catechism and creed. The former may be relatively unreflective or may have been subjected to reflection between the first and the second naiveté. It is the tradition which shapes the world view of ordinary people, has a logic and structure of its own, and at various times and places may have only a tenuous connection with the high tradition—often because only a tenuous connection is either possible or necessary (in the era, for example, when most Christians were illiterate peasants living in isolated villages).

The latter is the version of the story told by religious adepts, leaders, thinkers, teachers, philosophers, and theologians. It is systematic, rationalized (given its first principles), elaborate, detailed, reflective, precise, prosaic, and formal. It may often be boring, but it is necessary and not merely a necessary evil, necessary because humans must reflect on their experiences and find (what seem to be) rational grounds for accepting them. It is also necessary so that some group of deputized decision makers within the community have final authority to determine whether a given version of the story is truly compatible with the heritage. To put the matter somewhat differently, the two traditions must critique one another; the popular tradition will critique the high tradition for what often seems its bloodlines and arid rationality, and the high tradition will critique the popular tradition for its wildness, its unrestrained emotion, its transient and self-deceiving enthusiasms. Without the watchful guidance of the high tradition, the popular tradition may slip over the boundaries which separate religion from magic; in the absence of the energy and vitality of the popular tradition, the high tradition will find itself talking to empty churches or meeting houses.

I distinguish between the popular tradition and folk religion (and hence try to avoid the use of the confusing term "popular religion"). Folk religion is a mixture of the stories of a religious tradition with stories of preexisting animistic or magical traditions, a blending of which the elaborately poetic traditions like Catholicism or Hinduism seem especially prone, but from which no tradition of any of the world religions is immune. In the absence of effective conversation between the high tradition and the popular tradition, folk religion is probably inevitable.

Moreover, it is one of the primal insights of the sociological tradition that Catholics are different—or at least were different at the times when Durkheim noted the lower Catholic suicide rates and Weber observed the lower advanced school attendance rates. Catholics seemed then to be more "communal" than Protestants who were more likely to emphasize individual freedom in matters religious. In fact, the more accurate way of putting the matter might have been that Protestants were different, since religious individualism was an innovation that the Reformation introduced into the human condition. Whether these differences persist is a matter of some debate. It remains to be seen, however, that the different emphases reported at the beginning of this century by the founders of sociology have truly disappeared.

David Tracy in his study of the "classics" of the Protestant and Catholic heritages (*Analogical Imagination*, Crossroad, 1982) has described differences in the Catholic and Protestant imaginations which I will use as auxiliary tools for my theory. Catholicism tends to be more mystical, Protestantism more prophetic; Catholicism tends to emphasize the manifestation of God's goodness, Protestantism tends to emphasize the proclamation of God's judgment. Catholicism tends to emphasize God's presence in the world, Protestantism tends to emphasize God's absence from the world. Catholicism tends to the liberal use of metaphor to describe God (God is like . . .) while Protestantism is wary of the abuse that metaphor can cause (God is NOT like . . .). Hence, Catholicism indulges in such religious artifacts as angels, saints, holy souls, Mary the Mother of Jesus, stained glass windows, statues, elaborate processions, ornate vestments, holy water, votive candles, and all the other devotions and practices which the classical reformation theory abhorred as idolatry.

Tracy calls the Catholic imagination "analogical" and the Protestant imagination "dialectical" because the former says God is like . . . and the latter says God is NOT like. . . . Neither style, he contends, is better than the other. Both are part of the Christian heritage and essential to it. Neither heritage has a monopoly on its own style. In individual members both styles may well be combined. But there is a different emphasis nonetheless on the way God, world, human nature, and human community are pictured in the two religious imaginations. In developing my theory of the poetry of religion, I kept open the possibility that Catholics may still have more vivid religious imagery and that the Catholic heritage may well be what has been called a rain forest of metaphors.

In brief summary of other research I have done on the religious imagination, I have found that on a four-item scale designed to measure respondents' images of God (and hence to detect their religious stories) Catholics were more likely to lean in the direction of seeing God as Spouse, Lover, Mother, and Friend then were other Americans (and particularly than American Protestants) and that this different view of God and the world accounts for different attitudes among Catholics on social and political matters, including concern for the environment and sympathy for AIDS victims. Might it be possible, I asked myself, that the experiences, images, stories, community, and ritual which seem to lurk behind these higher scores on what I have come to call a GRACE scale have an impact at least on the Catholic popular tradition's treatment of sexual love? Might Catholics be more likely to, in effect, take St. Paul seriously when he suggested that the spouse is a sacrament of God?

Sex and the Married Catholic:
The Shadow of St. Augustine

In this chapter I will use my theory of the narrative and experiential nature of religion to explore the impact of negative Catholic sexual teaching on the behavior of American Catholics. How can it be that a religion whose members have higher scores on a scale made up of such measures as lover and spouse are so sexually inhibited? What happens when two religious stories are in conflict?

If they really are.

It is virtually axiomatic that the negative sexual teachings of the Catholic Church interfere with the marital pleasures of Catholic husbands and wives. How could it be otherwise? Has not the official Church since the time of St. Augustine insisted that even between husband and wife sex was essentially for procreation? Did not Augustine say that even sex between husband and wife, even when it was directed towards the procreation of children, was at least a small sin because of the loss of control? Did not the Pontifical Commission on the Family warn in the 1970s that husbands and wives should beware of the risks of "unbridled lust" in their marriage relationship? Does not even the new "personalist" approach to married sex of the last two Popes, so praised by some Catholic theologians, emphasize restraint rather than passion to say nothing of abandon? Have not the heads of younger Catholics for generations been filled with a mixture of ignorance and superstition, fear and anxiety about sex? How could Catholics not have more sexual hang-ups than other Americans? Do patent leather shoes . . . etc. etc.

One might well be written off as a fool for questioning such an analysis. We read in fiction and nonfiction, we hear stories from both those who have left the Church in disgust and those who hang on inside its boundaries, of the terrible agony that Catholic sexual teaching has created for those who have been exposed to it. I do not question either the authenticity or the pain of such experiences. But I remain to be convinced of their typicality—if only because I remain skeptical about whether men and women could have lived married lives together during the last fifteen hundred years under the shadow of St. Augustine's negative view of human sexuality. Indeed how many husbands and wives or their parish clergy have read St. Augustine or papal encyclicals or statements of the national hierarchies or instructions of the Congregation for the Defense of the Faith?

TWO TRADITIONS

So I propose to ask if there might have been another source by which Catholic insights on sex between husband and wife might have passed on down through the ages, a source which did not know Augustine and viewed passion between husband and wife with much more tolerance. To accomplish this task, I intend to use my sociological model of two traditions—the "High Tradition" and the "Popular Tradition"—and then fashion some hypotheses which can be tested against empirical data about the relative impact of the two traditions.

The High Tradition is the Catholicism one learns in schools; the Popular Tradition is the Catholicism one learned in great part before one went to school. The former is contained in the teaching of theologians and the Magisterium.[1] It is cognitive, propositional, didactic. It is

20

Catholicism in prose. The Popular Tradition is contained in the teaching of parents, family, neighbors, and friends. It is imaginative, experiential, narrative. It is Catholicism in poetry.

All of the world religions have both kinds of traditions, because all have their prose and poetic versions. Note for example in the the prose history of the Books of Kings and Samuel and the poetry of Isaia and the Song of Songs. Of the four religions of the Book (Judaism, Protestantism, Catholicism and Islam), Catholicism has the most richly developed popular tradition because it is least afraid of the possible idolatry imaginative dimension of religion. It is, to say the same thing in different words, the most sacramental of the four religions, the one most likely to see the transcendent lurking in the objects, events, and people of creation. It is the least likely to be afraid of contaminating God by using creation as a metaphor with which to describe Her.

If the High Tradition is to be found in theology books, the documents of the Councils and the Papacy, and various hierarchies of the world, the Popular Tradition is to be found in the rituals, the art, the music, the architecture, the devotions, the stories of ordinary people. If the former can be stated concisely at any given time in creeds which are collections of prose propositions, the latter is more fluid, amorphous, illusive and is expressed in stories.

Prosaic people that they are, the members of the Catholic elite are inclined to believe that the real Catholicism is that of the High Tradition. Doctrine and dogma are more important than experience and narrative. Literacy and education, they assume, will shortly dominate religion, and all but the elderly will realize that the religion of image and story is but a step above superstition.

The Christmas Crib is Popular Catholicism, the Decrees of Chalcedon on the meaning of that event are High Catholicism. The same story of God among humans is told by both, the same fundamental reality of the faith is disclosed by both, the same rumor of angels is heard in both. Which, however, has more impact on the lives of ordinary Catholics? Anyone who thinks *homoousios* is more important than the Madonna and her Child is incurably prosaic—besides being wrong!

The Popular Tradition is more than just popular devotions; even in the Popular Tradition the Eucharist is, for example, more than just the Feast of Corpus Christi (currently unfashionable), Corpus Christi processions, and visiting churches on Holy Thursday evening. The Eucharist is, to risk translating poetry into prose, God among humans at a family meal.

In its essence, the Popular Tradition, to risk again translating poetry into prose, asserts in the words of the Country Priest in George Bernanos's novel that everything is grace.

Including sex.

"Love is our origin, love is our constant calling, love is our fulfillment in heaven," says the liturgy of wedding Mass. "The love of man and woman is made holy in the sacrament of matrimony and becomes the mirror of your everlasting love."

It's very hard to think of that kind of love as at least somewhat sinful.

Only in this century of universal education and literacy has the High Tradition made a serious attempt to impose its Augustinian vision of the role of sexual love in marriage on the laity. Before that, their attitudes towards married love, one may suspect, was shaped by the Popular Tradition, a (sometimes just barely) Christianized version of paganism—which included the rings and the crowns and the gift of the bride by the father. Married love was good, it reflected God's love for us, husbands and wives should respect one another and treat each other as equals (more or less) and be grateful for the pleasures of sexual love. Augustine was heard neither in palace or hovel and often not even by the clergy who were poorly educated if not completely illiterate. The Popular Tradition flourished. Moreover, it was reinforced by the sacramentality of Catholicism which in the "popular" environment was not inhibited by Augustine's shadow. So marriage beds were blessed to hallow the sexual love between bride and groom and no one thought it strange, and the bride was blessed that she might be pleasing and vigorous in bed in the Sarum ritual.

How does one find the Popular Tradition on marital sex? Since by definition it is not written down in books, it is usually not easy to find, even at the present time, though it is pervasive and its influence powerful. One must search the marriage rituals and blessings, the manuals for confessors, popular sermons on married love, love poetry and cemetery epitaphs, parish documents and registers, and passing allusions in such documents as *Parsifal, The Divine Comedy*, and *The Canterbury Tales*. Though most of the monographic research has yet to be done or even begun, even cursory consideration demonstrates that the Popular Tradition did not buy the Augustinian perspective. One need only compare the attitude on sexual love of Wolfram von Eschenbach (the author of *Parsifal*) with that of Augustine to realize that the two men lived in different worlds when the subject was the love between man and woman.

How is the Popular Tradition transmitted? Through ritual and story, through song and dance, through priestly advice, through the instructions of one generation to another in the home, family, and village, and especially on the subject of sex, through the advice mothers gave their daughters, through the religious ambiance in which people lived. While these transmission mechanisms may seem weak and problematic, they are in fact, taken together, extraordinarily strong. If the Popular Tradition has dominated for most of Catholic history— and I argue that it has—the reason is that it was almost completely undisputed and indeed reinforced by the sacramental imagination of Catholicism.

The essence of this tradition on married love is, to use modern terminology, that sexual pleasure heals the frictions and conflicts of the common life and reinforces the bond between husband and wife. Not to understand this truth, married men and women down through the ages would have argued, is not to understand anything at all about marriage. Then and now their parish clergy tended to agree with them (and the "now" part of that assertion can be proved with empirical data).

No Hang-ups?

Is it not possible that the Augustinian theory of marital sex has no impact on Catholic behavior? Is it, to go one step further, that, should there be a Popular tradition, it might have a positive impact of Catholic sexual behavior? Therefore, it is appropriate to examine the hypothesis that Catholic sexual behavior in marriage is no more inhibited by the High Tradition than is the sexual love of anyone else and in fact may be reinforced by the sacramentality of the Popular Tradition. Catholic sexual hang-ups, in other words, may be no worse than anyone else's.

This analysis will be based on two representative samples of American married people (one with 1325 cases from my study of American marriage and the other with 4414 cases from the General Social Survey sexual behavior questions asked between 1989 and 1991). The latter will provide data about frequency of sexual intercourse which will provide the solid skeleton of my analysis, while the latter will, as it were, put flesh on the bones by offering information about sexual playfulness. I propose to test these indicators:

1. Frequency of sexual intercourse.

2. Persistence of sexual intercourse as one grows older.

3. Sexual playfulness: a scale combining such matters as prolonged periods of sexual play between spouses, mutual undressing, showers or baths together, swimming in the nude with one's spouse, making love outdoors, purchase of erotic undergarments, and experimentation with various sexual techniques.

4. A stronger Catholic effect in marriages where both partners are Catholic.

5. The strength of the correlation between frequency of intercourse and psychological well-being and personal happiness, an indirect measure of the "enjoyment" of sexual intercourse.

6. The strength of the correlation between frequent sex and marital satisfaction as measured by the response that one would marry the same spouse again if one had a chance to do it again, a second indirect measure of the "delight" in the spouse.

In the logic of my argument three outcomes are possible:

1. If Catholic scores are lower than those of others, the Catholic High Tradition has inhibited Catholic sexual activity: Catholics have more sexual hang-ups on the average than others.

2. If Catholic sexual behavior on these six indicators is no different from that of other Americans, it would follow that the High Tradition has at least not inhibited married sex among Catholics. Catholics have no more sexual hang-ups than anyone else, perhaps because the High Tradition no longer has any effect on their behavior, if it ever did.

3. If Catholic scores are on the average higher than those of others—which is what my model of a separate and more sexually positive Popular Tradition would lead me to expect—then Catholics must have fewer sexual hang-ups than others; be less inhibited sexually, especially if they are married to other Catholics; Catholics would seem to enjoy sex more than others do, particularly, to add a seventh indicator, those who have a "spousal" image of God. If religion is a story of a passion and loving relationship with God, might not that story affect the story of human passion with one's spouse?

The hypothesis based on my model of a Popular Tradition that Catholics are more sexually playful and have more sex than other Americans would be enough to get me laughed out of most dinner parties in this country. Everyone knows that it can't possibly be true that Catholics don't have more sexual hang-ups than other people. Right? Only a fool would suggest that Catholic married people are more sexually liberated than other Americans. Right? Any theory which would lead to such an absurd suggestion ought not to be taken seriously. Right?

Nonetheless, my findings are as follows:

1. Sixty-eight percent of the Catholics as opposed to 56% of the others engage in sexual union at least once a week. Catholics are significantly more likely to have sex weekly or more often than all others combined and also more likely to have sex frequently than are Liberal and Fundamentalist Protestants.

2. Frequency of intercourse declines with age but less precipitously among Catholics than among others so that Catholics are one quarter again more likely than others to have sex at least once a week when they are fifty-five years or older (50% versus 40%).

3. Catholics—especially Catholic women—score significantly higher on the sexual playfulness scale (Figure 1). For example, Catholics are half again as likely (three out of ten as opposed to two out of ten) to say they have purchased erotic undergarments either often or sometimes (Figure 2). They are also significantly more likely (Figure 3) to report showers or bath with their spouse.

4. On all three of these measures, the effect is strongest in endogamous Catholic marriages.

Are Catholics telling the truth about their sexual behavior? The ones in the best position to answer that question are the spouses of Catholics who themselves are not Catholic. The first testimony on what its like to have a spouse who is supposed to be living a sex life in the shadow of St. Augustine is to be found in Figure 4. Those Protestants who are married to Catholics are more likely to report intercourse once a week or more than are those Protestants married to other Protestants, Jews, members of other religions, and those with no religious affiliation.

Moreover, it is precisely Protestant men who report more frequent intercourse with Catholic wives than wives who themselves are Protestant. Finally, while the purchase of erotic lingerie is most likely to be reported in marriages in which both spouses are Catholic, it is more likely to be reported in a mixed marriage than it is in marriages in which neither partner is Catholic

5. The correlation between frequency of inter-course and personal well-being is .06 for others and .12 for Catholics: marital happiness corre-lates with sexual frequency at .18 for Catholics and .12 for others. Catholics "enjoy" sex more. Figure 5 shows that psychological well-being is only somewhat affected by frequency of sex for those who are not Catholics but strikingly and significantly affected for Catholics. Catholics who have sex infrequently are lower in personal happiness than others, and Catholics who have sex frequently are higher than others on personal happiness. Moreover, to anticipate, this special Catholic correlation is observed ONLY among those Catholics who imagine God as a spouse.

6. The correlation between frequency of inter-course and the response that one would marry the same spouse again is .15 for those who are not Catholics and .32 for those who are. Catholics who have sex infrequently are lower in this delight in the spouse than are others,

27

and Catholics who have sex frequently are higher in this delight in the spouse than others. The "delight" is even stronger among Catholic women than among Catholic men. Do Catholics really take such delight in a sexually active and erotically playful marital partner? The same significant correlation observed in Figure 5 for Catholics between frequent sex and satisfaction with the partner is indicated by the response that one would marry the same spouse again if one had to do it all over. In log linear analyses of the data, the preferred model is the one that contains the interaction between Catholicism and frequent sex.

7. Furthermore, in the GSS the image of God as spouse rather than master *accounts* completely for the difference between Catholics and other Americans in frequency of sex. Catholics have higher rates of sexual love because of the impact on them of the story of human marital passion as a hint of divine marital passion (Figure 6). For others, the spousal image has no significant effect on frequency of marital sex—one more interaction which shows that Catholics continue to be different, if not in the direction many would have thought when sexuality is the matter at issue.

8. Finally, the sexual playfulness scale (which exists in only the *Faithful Attraction* data) accounts completely for the higher intercourse rate of Catholics. In sociological terms, in a regression equation the playfulness scale reduces the difference in intercourse rates to statistical insignificance. Catholics engage in intercourse more frequently, it would seem, *because* they approach sex more playfully. Also, Catholic rates of sexual playfulness are especially high if

they have gracious images of God, that is, if they see benign human relationships (mother, spouse, friend, lover) as metaphors of God.

The model of the two traditions predicts that Catholics have sex more often, they are more playful in their sexual encounters, and they enjoy sex more. The predictions turn out to be accurate.

Stories of human passion seem for Catholics to both mirror and reflect stories of divine passion. In the absence of the prism of my theory of religion as poetry, it would have been most improbable that in addressing questions of Catholic marital relations I would have paid any attention to spousal imagery and its effect on Catholic married people. Indeed, the questions would not have even been in the General Social Survey if it were not for the theory.

Greater Catholic sexual playfulness—even sexual abandon—seems to be especially likely for Irish Catholic women who are more likely than any others to report that they often or sometime abandon all their sexual inhibitions, thus challenging the myth of the pious and frigid Irish virgin.[2]

CONCLUSION

These findings will offend two groups of people—those who desperately want to believe that most Catholics are suffering terribly because of the Church's sexual teaching and that therefore the Church is coming apart; and those Church leaders who still see married sex through the eyes of St. Augustine and want to warn the lay people of the dangers of unbridled lust. Neither response comprehends the durability, the pervasiveness, the influence, or the appeal of the Popular Tradition—that poetry of Catholicism which keeps most Catholics in the Church.

I do not argue that St. Augustine's fears about loss of control are invalid. One need merely read the stories in the daily papers or watch the evening news to understand that humans do terrible harm to other humans because of the sexual drive. Sex is potentially both demonic and tragic, indeed both the demonic and the tragic aspects of sexuality affect the personality of each of us. The Popular Tradition arguably underestimates the dangers, but it has surely protected the Catholic laity from married lives in St. Augustine's somber shadow.

Those who complain that a distinctive Catholic sexual ethic is disappearing might well contemplate the results: Catholics have sex more frequently, they are more playful in their sexual behavior, and they enjoy it more. It is not, one suspects, the difference that will please the complainers.

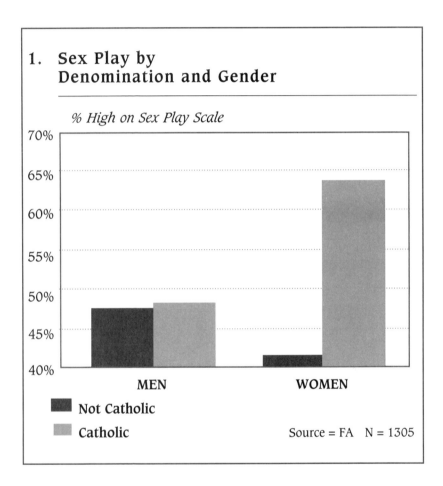

1. **Sex Play by Denomination and Gender**

% High on Sex Play Scale

Not Catholic
Catholic

Source = FA   N = 1305

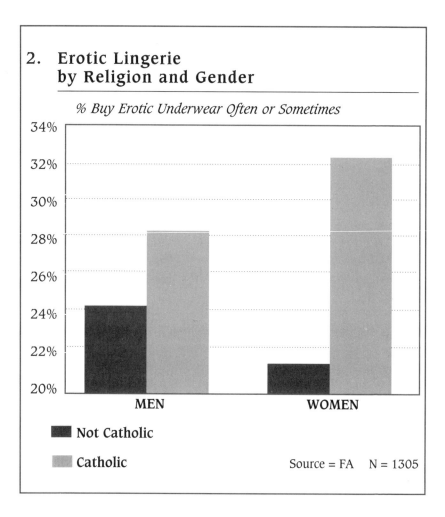

2. **Erotic Lingerie by Religion and Gender**

% Buy Erotic Underwear Often or Sometimes

MEN   WOMEN

■ Not Catholic

▨ Catholic

Source = FA   N = 1305

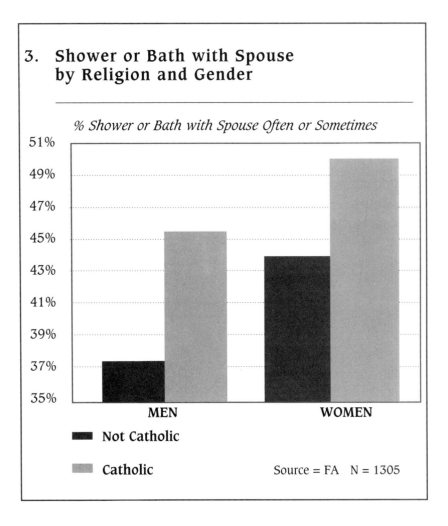

3. **Shower or Bath with Spouse by Religion and Gender**

% Shower or Bath with Spouse Often or Sometimes

51%
49%
47%
45%
43%
41%
39%
37%
35%

MEN   WOMEN

■ Not Catholic

▨ Catholic   Source = FA   N = 1305

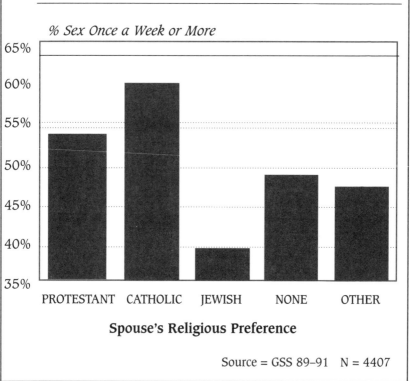

4. Frequency of Sex for Protestants by Spouse's Religion

% Sex Once a Week or More

| | PROTESTANT | CATHOLIC | JEWISH | NONE | OTHER |

Spouse's Religious Preference

Source = GSS 89–91   N = 4407

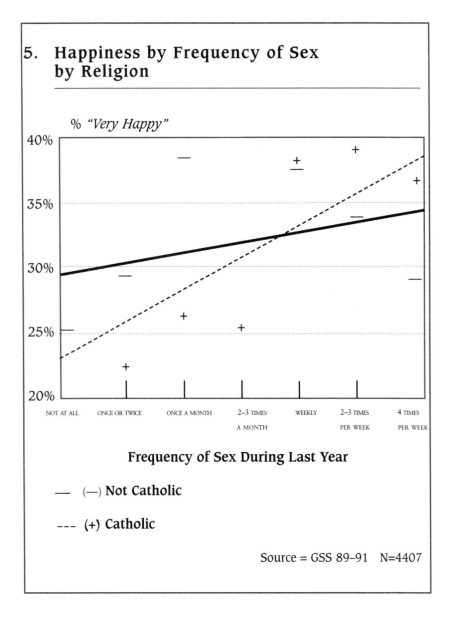

5. Happiness by Frequency of Sex by Religion

% *"Very Happy"*

Frequency of Sex During Last Year

— (—) Not Catholic

--- (+) Catholic

Source = GSS 89–91   N=4407

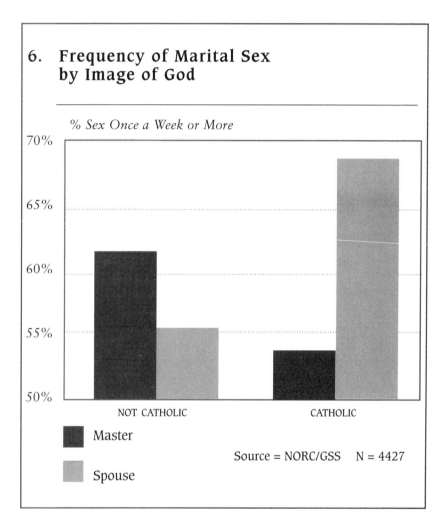

6. **Frequency of Marital Sex by Image of God**

% Sex Once a Week or More

- 70%
- 65%
- 60%
- 55%
- 50%

NOT CATHOLIC   CATHOLIC

- Master
- Spouse

Source = NORC/GSS   N = 4427

Birth Control and the Catholic Marriage: A Historical Perspective

During the "celebrations" of the twenty-fifth anniversary of *Humanae Vitae*, Pope Paul VI's 1968 birth control encyclical, Michael Novak admitted in the magazine *Crisis* that he had changed his mind because when he looked around at the "progressive couples I used to know . . . I don't see the marital bliss or sexual balance or even sexual health, whose arrival I used to anticipate once progressivism would finally take hold."

To say the least, such an argument is based on an interesting form of logic.

None of the celebrants of the twenty-fifth anniversary of the encyclical, however, have seemed troubled to inquire about the social and demographic history of contraception in the Catholic community. Nor has there been any effort to understand how the problem arose and how Catholics have responded to it. It is nonetheless possible through the use of survey data from thirty years ago to reconstruct some of that history and understand the nature of the crisis it created in the Catholic community.

The issue for this book is how the Catholic sexual experience as described in the last chapter managed to survive—if survive it did—the birth control rules which, as we shall see, were enforced so vigorously from 1930 to 1960.

The declining infant mortality rate created the birth control issue. Until the middle of the last century in parts of Western Europe and until the beginning of the present century in the rest of Europe, unlimited fertility was not a problem because the infant mortality rate diminished the number of children who would live to be adults. Indeed, more than seven pregnancies were required to produce two adults who would replace the parents in the population. Moreover, children were a substantial economic asset in an agricultural society because they were potential workers on the family farm.

But when elementary health measures brought down the infant mortality (and maternal death) rates, a woman could easily produce anywhere from eight to twelve children depending on her diet, her state of health, and the age of her marriage. Moreover, this change—which demographers call the demographic transition—happened almost overnight as human history goes. And at the same time, large migrations to the city were taking place and turning children from an economic asset to an economic cost of eventually very large proportions. The populations knew of ways to control fertility (infanticide, abortion, coitus interruptus) and have used them during previous times when there were too many children and too little food. While the local clergy may have condemned these practices (or perhaps merely ignored them), the Church hardly saw them as a matter for serious international concern, even should the means of transportation and communication have been available to lay down an international policy.

As John T. Noonan, Jr., observed in his classic book on the subject, *Contraception* (Harvard U. Press, 1986), French Catholics, among the first to be faced with the problem, responded with *coitus interruptus* (and it would seem, the invention of the condom). Several times the French hierarchy secretly asked Rome for advice on the problem. Each time they were told not to trouble the consciences of the laity. St. John Vianney, the Curé of Ars, in his conferences for confessors, repeated the advice, often in fierce language. Pope Leo XIII in his encyclical on marriage, written precisely at the time that contraception was widespread in France (and he knew it to be because of the questions of the French bishops), said nothing on the subject.

It is hard to believe that this kind of response did not represent the wisdom of previous practice. The Church at that time could not have suddenly acquired a horror of troubling the consciences of the laity. Rather it was probably following its traditional pastoral procedures, perhaps reinforced by the attitude on marriage matters of St. Alphonsus Liguori.

It is not absolutely clear how this wisdom was abandoned between Leo XIII in *Arcanum* and Pius XI in *Casti Connubii* (1930), between the Curé of Ars (1786-1859) warning against troubling the conscience of the laity to Cardinal George William Mundelein's order to his priests in the 1930s to question everyone who had been away from confession for more than six months about birth control. Surely by the middle 1930s, priests in the United States, Ireland, England, and Canada (at least) had moved from a policy of not troubling the consciences of the laity to troubling them as much as possible.

Judge Noonan suggests that Arthur Veermersch, S.J., who drafted *Casti Connubii* for Pius XI, insisted on including the passage on contraception in part because he felt a response was necessary to the Lambeth Conference's tolerance for birth control and in part because he feared that many priests were not enforcing the doctrine in the confessional. It would appear that the fateful words were added to the encyclical at the last moment.

Perhaps the reason for the reversal of practice was that by the early third of the twentieth century the demographic transition had affected so many countries that contraception seemed to have become universal. Nonetheless, it might have been useful if the Pope had been able to listen to the practical experience of those priests who were reluctant to trouble the consciences of the laity.

It would seem that in the southern European countries, the Church's condemnation of birth control was not and is not taken seriously by either clergy or laity. The wisdom of the Curé of Ars seems to have prevailed. However, in northern Europe it surely was taken seriously—from which it does not follow incidentally that it was ever effectively enforced.

However, in the United States (and presumably all the other English-speaking countries) *Casti Connubii* signaled the beginning of a fierce campaign of troubling the consciences of the laity.

There is only impressionistic and anecdotal data about clerical behavior in the United States between the First World War and the Second Vatican Council. My impression is that, with some notable and noisy exceptions, most of the parish clergy avoided preaching on the subject and handled it gingerly and sympathetically in the confessional. Cardinal Mundelein's order was apparently ignored by most Chicago confessors. However, the wandering missionaries (especially Redemptorists) and retreat masters periodically stirred up all kinds of trouble in the consciences of the laity—especially the former in the separate sessions for men and women.

My colleague, Ms. Ellen Skerrett, points out to me that much of the concern Catholic leaders and writers expressed in the late 1930s was about "race suicide"[1]—that is, the decline of the "white race." Indeed *Commonweal* praised Cardinal Mundelein in an article in 1939 for his successful campaign to prosecute in court the circulation of birth control literature. In words that subsequent editors of the journal probably wish no one would remember, they lauded Mundelein for opposing the birth control movement because "if the movement succeeded it might mean the end of the white races."

Mundelein's order apparently did not survive his death in 1940. Priests in the seminary at that time still heard that they should obey his order. Only ten years later my generation did not hear a word about it. Indeed, after listening to the arguments against birth control, we were given a way out in confessional practice—almost as a footnote. If one partner insisted on intercourse in which contraceptives were used, the other partner might consent for the good of the marriage, so long as she/he did not initiate the lovemaking interlude but only passively accepted it. We were not to preach this conclusion and indeed should only tell the laity about it in the confessional and extract a promise of secrecy from them. In a complicated fashion we did not understand—especially since we had not heard of his conferences—this approach was an invitation to return to the wisdom of the Curé of Ars.

"When you say 'passive,'" someone asked, "do you mean the partner cannot enjoy the lovemaking?" The professor responded with something like, "you gotta be kidding."

"That's the end of game," I remember saying after class. "It's finished."

I have no way of knowing how many priests actually used that escape hatch. Only in retrospect do I understand how ingenious it was, given the intensity of the anti-birth-control sentiment in the Church at that time. I suspect that we didn't realize how wide the escape hatch was.

If I had to speculate about the history of the four-decade-long attempt to trouble the consciences of the laity, I would guess that it reached its high water mark in 1944 when the Holy Office under Pius XII reaffirmed the teaching that procreation was the only primary end of marriage and that it was already in decline seven years later when the same Pope spoke sympathetically about responsible family planning and endorsed the still problematic rhythm method. It had spent its force, as NORC data I will shortly cite will demonstrate, by the early 1960s.

Nonetheless, in the 1940s, Bernard Lonergan, perhaps the greatest Catholic theologian of the twentieth century, turned away from work on the theology of marriage because an article in *Theological Studies* in 1943 was judged to be incompatible with the 1944 Holy Office declaration. The editor of Lonergan's works suggests that he had been influenced by the writings of two European theologians, Herbert Doms and Dietrich von Hildebrand, who were under an ecclesiastical cloud for suggesting that love between husband and wife was primary in marriage.

Dangerous radicals, clearly!

By the middle 1960s, in the NORC study of American priests, 67% of the respondents would not refuse absolution to lay people practicing birth control. Five years later, after *Humanae Vitae*, the overwhelming majority (87%) would not do so. Sixty percent of the clergy flatly rejected the birth control teaching. The Church's experiment in troubling the consciences of the laity had failed.

It therefore appears that for reasons of the demographic transition contraception became a major problem in the Church only in the early years of this century and ceased to be a problem for the laity and the lower clergy by the late middle years (1970).

I am not saying that the Church changed its teaching. Patently it did not. I am saying that the Church in the parishes returned to the practices of John Vianney. I doubt that all the encyclicals in the world could cause another reversal. Nor am I saying that this practice is the way things ought to be. I am merely saying as an empirical scholar that it is the way things are and are likely to continue to be.

I will also confess to being furious when I read Judge Noonan's book. My teachers had lied to me because they had not told the whole truth. Perhaps they did not know it. I remember citing Noonan to Archbishop Jadot and pointing out that Leo XIII had ignored contraception in *Arcanum*. He smiled, "Ah, you know about that encyclical, do you?"

Meanwhile, what was happening among the laity? There is a myth that at one time the good, pious lay people did not practice family limitation but had large families and trusted in God. In fact, that is not the case. Using data from the 1963 NORC[2] Catholic School Study, I calculated the completed fertility for Catholic married women in the sample. For those born before 1910, the rate was 3.4 children, for those born between 1910 and 1920 the rate was 3.2 children, and for those born in the 1920s the rate was 3.8 children. The middle group were for the most part in their childbearing years during the great depression and their lower rate may have been in substantial part due to a somewhat later age at marriage. Similarly the higher rate of the last group (the mothers of the baby boomers!) might well be the result of a somewhat earlier age of marriage.

Since unlimited fertility would have produced much larger families (six or more), one has to conclude that some form of birth control was used by Catholic women who were born even at the turn of the century.

Using a correction factor described by Samuel H. Preston,[3] I was able to project family size for Catholic women back to 1870: 4.34 for women born in the 1870s, 4.88 for those born in the 1880s, and 4.01 for those born in the 1890s. The somewhat higher rate for those born in the 1880s may be the result of the huge turn-of-the-century immigration. Many of the women in those years were not born in the United States.

Thus, Catholic family size diminished between 1870 and 1940, but only from 4.3 to 3.8. Large families were not typical even of women born in the last third of the last century. In Ireland at any rate, family size was controlled by late age of marriage. It is impossible even to speculate about the means of family limitation practiced by these women. Health and nutrition as well as later age of marriage and absent husbands (immigrants to America before their wives, or migratory workers in this country) might account for their fertility being less than one might expect.

But what about large Catholic families? Do not many American Catholics remember that their parents or grandparents came from large families? How is that memory compatible with the statistics which indicate families indeed larger than those of Protestants but still relatively small?

This phenomenon is the result of a mathematical paradox: many more people come from large families than there were large families. Thus, the descendants of large families are over-represented in the population compared to the number of families in which they were raised. Consider a population of six families, two of which have ten children, two of which have six, and two of which have three. That would mean thirty-eight children, more than half of which (twenty) would come from only two or one-third of the families.

Thus it appears that, as we peer back into the early years of this century through the prism of the 1963 Catholic School Study, we discover women who were practicing one way or another some form of family limitation.

The Church in effect gave women three choices: risk unlimited fertility, don't sleep with your husbands, stay away from the sacraments—a range of choices which might seem cruel.

But what about the "rhythm" method of family planning, as it was called in those days? One must remember that it was only approved as something to be tolerated by Pope Pius XII in 1951. In the middle 1930s it was often denounced by hard-liners. Ms. Skerrett pointed out that Dr. Leo Latz, a professor at Loyola Medical School, was denounced in an article in the Jesuit magazine *America* in February of 1933 because he wrote a book on rhythm and was "dropped" from Loyola Medical School. Nonetheless, the book became a bestseller (60,000 copies sold in the first year). Some priests secretly passed it out in rectory parlors.

Which of the three choices did Catholic women follow until the middle 1960s? Evidently most of them did not follow the choice of having as many children "as God gives us." Doubtless some of them did indeed withdraw from sexual relations (on occasion perhaps with a sigh of relief). Others— I suspect most of them—practiced some form of "artificial" birth control and stayed away from the sacraments. Some surely defied the Church and practiced birth control but did not confess it. I have the impression (from my experience as a confessor in those days) that many combined the second and the third approach: they chose a form of birth control other than "rhythm" and confessed it when they went to confession at Christmas or Easter or First Communion even though they knew that they would shortly return to the forbidden method. Again my impression is that few priests were willing to make an issue of such confessions. You gave them absolution and sent them away in God's peace.

The work of demographer Charles Westoff[4] provides a snapshot of the behavior of Catholic women in the fifties and sixties. In 1955, 30% of Catholic women in their childbearing years were using some form of "artificial" birth control. In 1960, the rate had risen to 38%, and in 1965 to 53%. For those who were regular churchgoers, the rates were not greatly different: 22%, 31%, and 44%. In reinterviews in 1969 (the year after *Humanae Vitae*) the rate was 64%.

I conclude from these data that pressures were building up inside the Catholic community against the birth control teaching before the Second Vatican Council and that even without the Council, without the papal commission established by Pope John (whose findings Pope Paul overruled), and possibly even without the "pill" (which substituted for rhythm among Catholic women in the early and middle sixties according to Westoff), changes in attitudes and behavior among both the lower clergy and the laity would have occurred in the middle and late sixties and that no encyclical, not even one which was not tardy, would have prevented the change.[5]

I now turn to more data from the 1963 study to determine what Catholic women were thinking about birth control just as the Council had begun and just as the "pill" was becoming available. I will use eight graphs to compare attitudes of the various birth cohorts of Catholic women at that time with the subsequent attitudes of the same cohorts eleven years later in the 1974 NORC Catholic School Study. I note in passing that the data from the two studies are now an important historical resource for depicting Catholicism in the United States for those two decades; I remain surprised that no one asks for copies of the data set for research purposes. Perhaps the data are tainted by the reactions from both Catholic left and right.

The latter condemned the two studies for not supporting the Pope, and the former ridiculed the findings and continues to do so.

Figure 1 depicts the response of Catholic women to a question about whether birth control was wrong.[6] The black line represents responses in 1963, the lighter, dashed-line responses in 1974. The codes at the bottom of the graph present the birth cohort (the year in which a respondent was born collapsed into decades). In this first graph we observe that not only do almost half of those born up to and including the 1930s believe that birth control is not wrong but that there is little change as one moves to the left across the cohort line except for the upswing in rejection of official doctrine among those born in the 1940s. Thus more than two-fifths of those born at the turn of the century and who would be well beyond their childbearing years at the time of the study rejected the official teaching. Eleven years later, rejection was massive in all cohorts. Not only did many of the young change their mind, so, too, did many of those for whom childbearing was no longer an issue.

In Figure 2, the dependent variable is a response to the question of whether the Church has the right to dictate the kinds of family limitation Catholics may use.[7] Clearly, the rejection of this right was massive by 1974. But even in 1963, almost half of Catholic women born before the 1930s also rejected this right. Does this represent a change from previous acceptance? We have no way of knowing for sure, but answers of those women who were born before 1910 suggests that reservations about the right of the Church in this area were not new in 1963.

Figures 3 and 4 consider responses by the various cohorts at both points in time to two attitudinal questions[8] which seemed to us at that time to reflect the ideology of some of the Catholic birth control teaching—sex was not supposed to be just for pleasure and trust in God's support if one had as many children as possible. From those born since 1910, the majority of Catholic women rejected both ideological positions—and opposition increased among the younger cohorts. For the older women did this represent a change from what they might have thought during their childbearing years? Or were their responses in 1963 consistent with what they always believed?

In the second set of four graphs, I turn to the attitudes on these issues of those "good" Catholics about whom the conservatives always want to hear—those who received Communion every week. Even a fifth of them did not agree with the Church on birth control, including a fifth of those born at the beginning of the century (Figure 5). Some thirty percent (Figure 6)—even of the oldest—did not think the Church had the right to specify birth control methods. Beginning with those born in 1920 (Figure 7), the majority of frequent communicants accept the notion that pleasure alone is sufficient reason for sex and only a slight majority of those born after 1910 think that they should have as many children as possible and trust in God (Figure 8).

Thus the Church had lost the support of the majority of Catholic women in their attitudes towards birth control and the purpose of sex in 1963—and arguably long before that—and was losing the support even of the most devout women, especially those born in the 1940s. As the broken lines on all eight charts demonstrate, the game was completely lost (to use the words I had spoken in the seminary in 1953) in all birth cohorts eleven years later.

Two facts stand out in all eight graphic portraits of American Catholic women during the 1960s and early 1970s. The first is how great was the change at all age levels in eleven short years. The second, and perhaps more striking because less appreciated even today, is how great was pressure for change in 1963. The balance was already tipping against the official position even then, even among women beyond their childbearing years. The gap between the two lines in my eight graphs—the increase in rejection during the eleven–year period—is in substantial part, I speculate, the result of the already high levels of rejection which existed in 1963. The trend towards rejection might have increased anyway, though perhaps more slowly, even if none of the astonishing events of that decade had not occurred. The "pill" alone is the only outside mechanism which one needs to postulate to account for the speed of the change. Ironically, the encyclical came too late. But even if it had not been so tardy, I doubt that the situation in 1974 would have been much different.

In summary, the Church began a serious campaign to talk large numbers of the faithful out of birth control only in this century (because only in this century was it perceived as a problem). The campaign to trouble the consciences of the laity became official in 1930 and was for all practical purposes over on the parish level forty years later. Let no one write this off as (in the words of the Pope's press officer) something that happened only in "an irresponsibly permissive society, hyper-inflated with sexuality," because it has happened, perhaps within a somewhat different time frame, in every European and North Atlantic country, including Ireland and Poland.

This summary however does not take into account the enormous amount of human suffering that the campaign imposed on the laity, especially on lay women. The choice imposed on them of no sex or no sacraments or no limitation on family size was a harsh one—and still is, even if it is not taken seriously by most Catholics. For many, many Catholic women, it would seem, the result was long years of troubled sex, anxious calendar watching, and infrequent reception of the sacraments. I am astonished that so few left the Church and virtually all returned to the sacraments when their child-bearing years were over. The Catholic heritage must have been extremely important to them. Apparently they loved the Church greatly despite what it had done to them.

Nonetheless, Church leaders have a lot to answer for, and their responsibility is all the more serious because so much of what they did and said was both arrogant and ignorant and done and said by men who had no personal involvement in the experiences about which they were making judgments. In their defense it may well be argued that they were caught in two demographic processes that no one understood at the time—the demographic transitions (declining infant mortality rates) and urbanization (children becoming an economic cost instead of an economic asset). Yet even today one finds few Church leaders who understand the importance of these changes.

I do not propose to argue in this context the ethical issue of the birth control prohibition. That is more properly left to the ethicians. I will be content with saying that Church leaders seemed to have missed some matters which might have made them less harsh and might have prevented a situation in which on the important issue of human sexuality they have lost all credibility.

Surely it is clear from the human sciences (of one of which I am a practitioner and hence may speak with authority) that it is natural for husband and wife to make love, one with another. Indeed what is uniquely human about human sexuality—in comparison with that of the other higher primates—is not its reproductive capabilities (the other higher primates reproduce without nearly as much fuss and bother as humans require) but its bonding capabilities. Uniquely and specifically, human sexuality is designed to bond the male and the female together so they can raise their offspring to adulthood. One might even contend that, given the friction and the conflict inherent in the close common life of a man and woman, the more and better the sex, the stronger will be the bonds that hold them together, all other things being equal. Under such circumstances from the point of view of the human sciences, it would seem to be unnatural (in the sense of weakening the natural bond between them) for them not to make love for long periods of time. Most married people will insist, if they are given half a chance, that sexual love is essential to hold a marriage together and that in its absence the ties between husband and wife tend to loosen and fray. If Catholic women in the four decades before 1963 continued to make love with their husbands despite the fact that such love seemed to bar them from the sacraments, the reason—as they would tell you again if given half a chance—was that sex was necessary if the marriage were to continue.

But the problem is that they were not permitted and are not permitted now that half a chance to speak of their experience of the bonding power of sexual love in marriage.

If excluding reproduction completely is in violation of the natural law, so excluding the healing and restorative powers of marital sex for a long period of time also would seem to be unnatural—and so might be glancing nervously at the calendar when reconciliation and renewal desperately need to be underwritten by passionate pleasure. Church leaders have all too easily dismissed this insistent and valid demand of nature.

The laity could have told Church leaders that. But no one asked them. The lower clergy could have told them the same thing, but no one asked them either. As far as that goes, no one is asking them now.

It is in this area of the bonding power of human love as something both unique to our kind of higher primate and also utterly and necessarily natural that there might be some possibility of dialogue towards clarification between the leaders of the Church on the one hand and laity and the lower clergy on the other. The Church has surely protected the pro-creative dimensions of married love, but one must ask whether it has not underestimated the equally "natural" bonding dimension. Can it not find a way to do both simultaneously?

One strives in vain to hear conversation on that subject. Surely there was nothing in the triumphalism of the *Humanae Vitae* celebration that gave a hint of the possibility of such dialogue. To say that the choice of no-sex, no-sacraments, or no-limitation seems harsh, cruel, and unnatural will offend those like who think that the Church must teach people to say "no." Some might feel that there is a possible middle ground between saying "yes" to promiscuity and "yes" to the binding power of marital love.

How does one explain the apparent sexual exuberance of Catholics in the late eighties and the early nineties against the background of sexual repression inherent in the policies of the Church in the era between 1930 and 1970?

My theory of the two traditions leads me to believe that the sacramental and the theological traditions were in deep conflict during that era. One of the reasons that the (Augustinian) theological tradition lost so completely was that its rigid application during those four decades was so much at odds with what Catholic lay people sensed (however preconsciously) in their imaginations. They knew that sex between husband and wife, indeed sexual pleasure between husband and wife, was not only good but holy. However much agony many of them may have suffered (and many suffered acutely), they were not about to abandon that instinct. That they did not leave the Church in vast numbers is evidence enough that they valued the Catholic religious sensibility and did not want to, indeed would not, give it up. Perhaps the sexual lives of many of them became more exuberant, more sacramental, more Catholic after the childbearing years were over. Perhaps those who made up their minds that the Church was wrong (as many had done long before the 1960s) enjoyed sex with their spouse the same way Catholics seem to do today—even if they felt that they could not receive the sacraments or could do so only by fudging a little in the confessional.

However the sacramental tradition was kept alive, it clearly did and is now resurgent again. Would the Catholic experience of sex have been even more exuberant it were not for the grim middle decades of this century? In truth, I don't know the answer to that question. Nonetheless, that the Catholic sacramental tradition of sex is still alive is a testimony to its remarkable durability. If the years between *Casti Connubii* and *Humanae Vitae* could not extinguish it, nothing can. If the leadership could not drive the married laity out of the Church in those years, one has to wonder what more they could do to empty the churches.

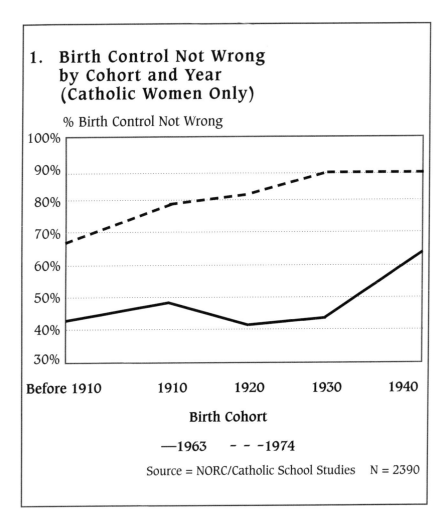

1. **Birth Control Not Wrong by Cohort and Year (Catholic Women Only)**

% Birth Control Not Wrong

Birth Cohort

—1963   - - -1974

Source = NORC/Catholic School Studies   N = 2390

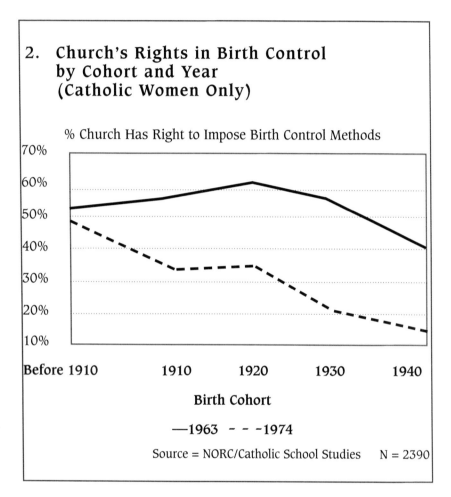

2. **Church's Rights in Birth Control by Cohort and Year (Catholic Women Only)**

% Church Has Right to Impose Birth Control Methods

70%
60%
50%
40%
30%
20%
10%

Before 1910   1910   1920   1930   1940

Birth Cohort

—1963   - - -1974

Source = NORC/Catholic School Studies   N = 2390

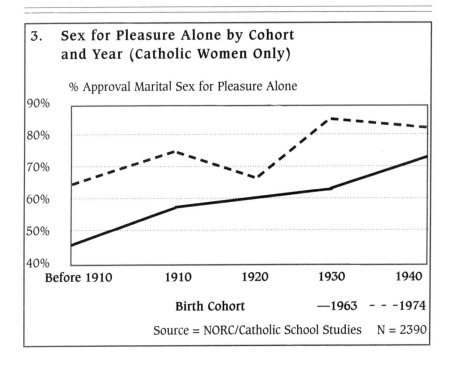

3. Sex for Pleasure Alone by Cohort and Year (Catholic Women Only)

% Approval Marital Sex for Pleasure Alone

Birth Cohort —1963 - - -1974

Source = NORC/Catholic School Studies   N = 2390

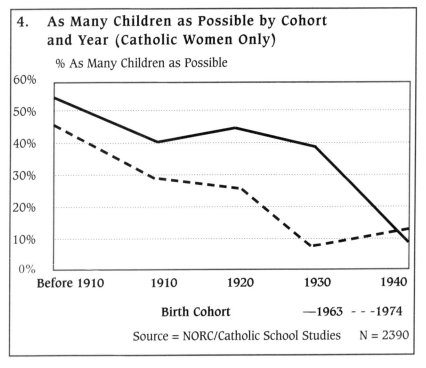

4. As Many Children as Possible by Cohort and Year (Catholic Women Only)

% As Many Children as Possible

Birth Cohort —1963 - - -1974

Source = NORC/Catholic School Studies   N = 2390

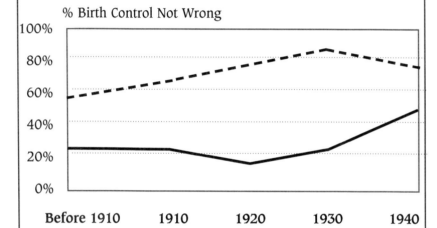

5. **Birth Control Not Wrong by Cohort and Year (Catholic Women Who Are Frequent Communicants)**

% Birth Control Not Wrong

100%				
80%				
60%				
40%				
20%				
0%				

Before 1910   1910   1920   1930   1940

Birth Cohort

——1963 - - -1974

"Frequent Communicants" = At Least 2 or 3 Times a Month

Source = NORC/Catholic School Studies   N = 788

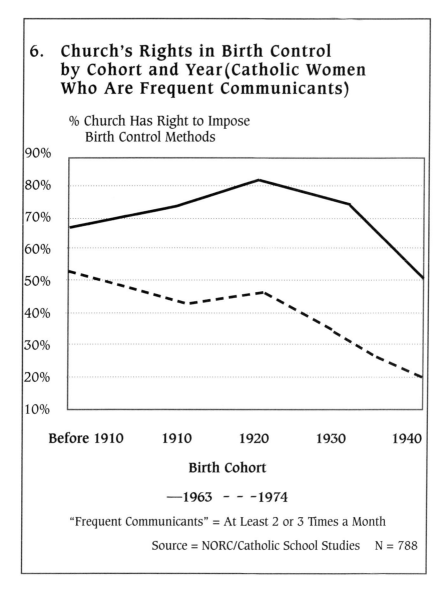

6. **Church's Rights in Birth Control by Cohort and Year (Catholic Women Who Are Frequent Communicants)**

% Church Has Right to Impose
Birth Control Methods

Birth Cohort

—1963 - - -1974

"Frequent Communicants" = At Least 2 or 3 Times a Month

Source = NORC/Catholic School Studies   N = 788

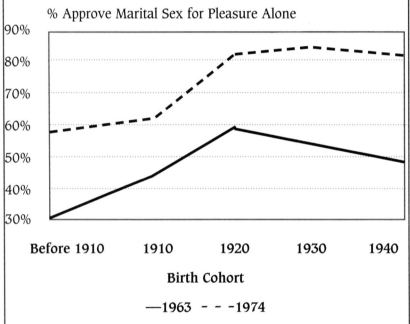

7. **Sex for Pleasure Alone by Cohort and Year (Catholic Women Only Who Are Frequent Communicants)**

% Approve Marital Sex for Pleasure Alone

90%
80%
70%
60%
50%
40%
30%

Before 1910   1910   1920   1930   1940

Birth Cohort

—1963 - - -1974

"Frequent Communicants" = At Least 2 or 3 Times a Month

Source = NORC/Catholic School Studies   N = 788

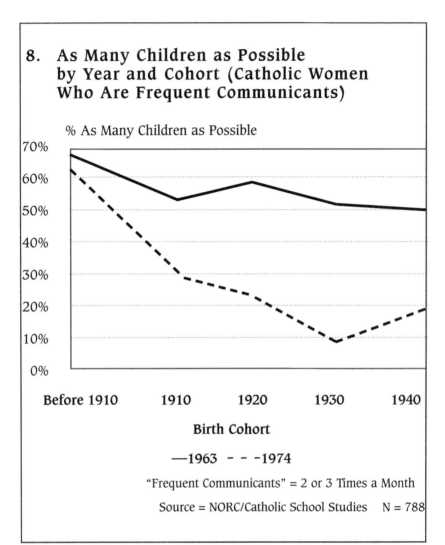

8. **As Many Children as Possible by Year and Cohort (Catholic Women Who Are Frequent Communicants)**

% As Many Children as Possible

70%
60%
50%
40%
30%
20%
10%
0%

Before 1910   1910   1920   1930   1940

Birth Cohort

—1963 - - -1974

"Frequent Communicants" = 2 or 3 Times a Month

Source = NORC/Catholic School Studies   N = 788

The Sacramental Spouse
As Metaphor for God

In this chapter, I propose to describe the spirituality of marriage organized around the metaphor of God-as-Spouse as it is to be found among the approximately one quarter of married Americans who experience their spouse as sometimes "like God." I make no claim that the experience which leads to the use of the spousal metaphor is typical or even the central metaphor for those who experience. Rather I wish to explore what experiences lead a man or a woman when presented with the poles of the metaphor "God" and "Spouse" to affirm a likeness between the two and then ask whether these experiences and the metaphor which represents them can contribute to understanding how we name God, a project reintroduced to religious discourse by the noted theologian, David Tracy. I seek to learn what are the contents of this metaphor as it is affirmed by married men and women—a probability sample of married men and women and not just married theologians (though the experiences of the latter are valuable too).

If it is true as Tracy argues that modernist names for God are still "deism, a warmer deism perhaps than the eighteenth century's but deism nonetheless," one must wonder whether the spousal image has become deistic.

RESEARCH STRATEGY

In a recent survey[1] of married Americans, respondents were asked whether the following applies to the spouse: "Sometimes like a god[2] to You." The possible answers are "Strongly applies," "Applies somewhat," "Does not apply."

The research strategy was not to ask the respondents why they could accept such a metaphor but rather to seek among the more than forty traits which were attributed to spouses the ones which distinguished between those who accepted the metaphor and those who did not. Thus, one probes the imaginations of respondents at the preconscious level without their knowing that one is trying to learn one of the names they use for God.

Metaphors, as St. Paul discovered to his syntactical discomfort, can work in both directions. Presumably the respondents who felt that their spouse was God-like knew God before they knew their spouse. Thus the primary direction of comparison would be that the spouse is like God. However, as St. Paul struggled to say, an intense and satisfying experience of the spouse might well influence the image of God so that God would be experienced as spouse-like. My wife, a male respondent might be saying, sometimes reminds me of God, but when I picture God I am sometimes reminded of her; so they both remind me of each other.

Patently, the wording of the question is not religious in the institutional sense. Yet experiences and metaphors are pre-institutional as well as preconscious—though they may later be reinforced (or weakened) by the response of the religious institution. All that matters for the purpose of this analysis is that when a married person is confronted with the image of God and the image of the spouse, the respondent perceives—preconsciously—that the two have enough in common that a likeness can be affirmed. God has been experienced, the spouse has been experienced, and the name "spouse" has been given to God. Fortunate respondent, fortunate spouse and, arguably, fortunate God.

Seven percent of American men and 4% of American women say that the metaphor applies strongly to their spouse; 16% of the men and 11% of the women say that the metaphor applies "somewhat" to their spouse. Hence, men are more likely to accept the metaphor (23%) than are American women (15%). Catholics are marginally more likely than Protestants (22% versus 20%). Are men more romantic (as the findings in *Faithful Attraction* would suggest)? Or are women more realistic than men? Or in fact are women more God-like than men? As the analysis progresses I will attempt to answer these questions.

The metaphor also correlates with age but in a peculiar fashion. For both men and women the propensity to endorse the metaphor declines after the early years of marriage until the age group between forty-five and fifty-years old and then rebounds among those over fifty-five. A technique called logistic regression established that the "U" curves are statistically significant. Is this curve a life cycle phenomenon? Does the spouse appear less godlike as age increases and then more God-like at the end of a life cycle, a classic love story phenomenon? Or have the birth cohorts (those who were born during the same span of years) currently in the middle years of life always been less likely to see their spouse as a metaphor for God? These questions cannot be answered with certainty without repeated surveys which follow a cohort through the life cycle. Nonetheless, it does seem likely that the image of God as spouse flourishes in both the earlier and the later years of marriage and declines during the middle years.

It should be noted here that the apparent resurgence of spousal imagery after the age of fifty-five cannot be explained by the departure from the pool of those married by divorce. The median duration of a marriage at time of divorce is six years so that the break-up of marriages which were not God-like would have occurred long before the age of fifty-five. So, too, would the remarriages of divorced people. Hence the phenomenon of decline and resurgence seems to be either life cycle or cohort—either a passage through which all marriages go or a lower level of use of the metaphor by those born between certain years—roughly between the middle 1930s and the late 1950s and early 1960s (the group the center of which would be the so-called baby boomers).

There were no reasons based on antecedent theory which would have justified predictions about what variables would correlate with the spousal metaphor. I had a hunch that the explanatory system might be different from that which would predict a "successful marriage."[3] Perhaps those variables which predicted a response that the marriage was "very happy," that the spouse was the respondent's "best friend," and that the respondent would marry the same spouse again if the choice were to be made now are not the same variables as those variables which predict that a respondent considers the spouse to be God-like.

POSSIBLE EXPLANATIONS

I sorted out twelve "factors" (clusters of variables which correlate one with another) which might correlate with the spousal metaphor and added three individual variables— frequency of sexual relations, the practice by spouses of prayer together, and the respondent's weight. A commonality of values and the quality of the relationship powerfully affected marital satisfactions as measured by the three characteristics mentioned in the previous paragraph.[4] Would these two sets of attributes also predict the comparison of the spouse to God?

The following is a description of the fifteen variables I used in the analysis (I usually ask colleagues and students when I am presenting these data to guess what the most powerful predictor of a God-like image of the spouse would be. Then I ask them to name the first three. The reader may wish to engage in the same exercise):[5]

MARRIAGE VALUES

Confidence in the stability of the marriage

Agreement on financial issues

Ability to disagree with each other without threatening the relationship

Agreement on basic values

Agreement on religious issues

Trust Spouse

SEXUAL VALUES

Sexual fulfillment

Quantity and quality of lovemaking

Sexual satisfaction

HOME VALUES

Hours of conversation per week

Spouse helps with household tasks.

Spouse is good with children.

QUALITY FACTOR

Is kind and gentle

Makes you feel important

Treats you as an equal

Delights in you

CHARM SPOUSE FACTOR

Is mysterious

Is exciting

Is a sharp dresser

Is romantic

SEXUAL FRUSTRATION FACTOR

Disappointed during sex

Spouse disappointed in sex

Spouse is not sexually frustrated.

SEXUALLY ATTRACTIVE FACTOR

Spouse is attractive.

Spouse is a skillful lover.

Spouse thinks respondent attractive.

Friends say respondent is attractive

EROTIC FACTOR

Spouses take shower or bath together.

Spouses swim in the nude together.

Spouses indulge in long periods of sexual play.

Spouses purchase erotic underwear.

Spouses watch erotic films.

Spouses experiment sexually.

NAKED FACTOR

Does not feel ashamed to be naked in presence
of spouse

Is not embarrassed by sex

Does not feel embarrassment during lovemaking

DISROBE FACTOR

Spouses take off each other's clothes

Enjoys undressing for spouse

GRACE FACTOR

God as Mother rather than Father

God as Spouse rather than Master

God as Lover rather than Judge

DEVOTION FACTOR

   Church attendance

   Prayer

   Spouses pray together

FREQUENCY OF SEX

SPOUSES PRAY TOGETHER

RESPONDENT'S WEIGHT

Findings: A Vivid Metaphor Indeed

The strongest predictors of the use of the spousal metaphor, net of one another and of all other variables, are CHARM, DISROBE and NAKED. Those most likely to think of their spouse as being like God are those who would describe the spouse as mysterious, exciting, romantic, and a sharp dresser,[6] those who enjoy undressing for their spouse and report that they undress one another, and those who are not embarrassed by nudity in the marriage relationship. Thus, a sharing of sexual values and the frequency of sexual intercourse are not predictors of the spousal metaphor, but the quality of the sexual relationship as described by enjoyment of bodily nudity and erotic playfulness are strong predictors (as social science predictors go). It is not so much the physical performance of sex as delight in the quality of the sexual ambiance that correlates with a God-like image of the spouse.

That the content of the metaphor of spouse and God would be so vivid and earthy, so powerfully erotic and so deeply physical, perhaps ought not to be a surprise. I for one, however, did not expect it.

Because the explanatory systems are so different for the two marriage outcomes, it does not follow that the sacramental spouse is a substitute for an ordinary happy marriage. Quite the contrary, those who consider their spouses to be God-like have significantly higher scores on all three measures—71% versus 61% for "very" happy marriage, 89% versus 82% for marriage to the same spouse, and 86% versus 74% for the spouse as best friend. Thus it would seem that a spouse who is comparable to God adds a payoff to marital happiness over and above that which exists on the average in marriages where the metaphor is not operative.

When the fourth and fifth most powerful predictors— sexual attractiveness and quality of the personal relationship—are added to the explanatory model, 16% of the variance in response to the spousal metaphor question can be accounted for by the model. In social research, multivariate explanations of such power are generally considered to be quite impressive. Four of the five factors involve sexuality, but none of them directly involves frequency of sexual inter- course. Clearly, God-like images are closely linked to the quality if not the quantity of the sexual lives of married people.

Thus far I have presented correlates of a God-like image of the spouse. I now turn to attempts at explaining some of the puzzles which have arisen in this presentation.

FURTHER EXPLORATIONS

The God-like image increases among those over fifty five and continues to correlate for them with the quality of sexual- ambiance. But can it be that those over fifty-five engage in nudity which seems to be correlate with the spousal image? A high score on the DISROBE factor does not decline with age for those who think of God as a spouse, but it falls from 50% to 20% for those who do not image their spouse as God-like. So for those who picture their spouse as a God, enjoyment of nudity, one's own and one's spouse's, does not decline with age but continues to be one of the joys of life.

Moreover, to look at the same relationship from another perspective, the proportion of those with high scores on the DISROBE factor who picture the spouse as like God actually increases dramatically with age, from 20% to almost 70%.

Whether sustained mutual nudity induces a God-like imagery or the imagery sustains the sexual reveling involved in such nudity is a question which cannot be answered with the present data. However, it is not unreasonable to assume that both sustain each other. Deism, even a warmer deism, this image surely is not.

Moreover, among those who picture their spouse as like God, there is no decline on the ATTRACTIVE factor with age but an increase, while for those who do not share that imagery there is a sharp decline on this factor which measures evaluation of self and spouse as good-looking and good lovers (as evaluated by the other). If one desegregates from the factor the item in which the respondent is asked to judge whether the spouse thinks the respondent is attractive, the proportion of women who feel their spouse finds them attractive increases from 60% to almost 90% with age for those who think their spouse is God-like; while for those who do not share this spousal imagery, the proportion who feel they are attractive to their spouses declines sharply.

Is this attractiveness merely in the eye of the beholder? Or can some women become more attractive with the passage of years? Or are the questions beside the point? If the God-like spouse is perceived as thinking his wife is attractive then that perception is all that matters; it may very well make her more attractive not only in his eyes but in the eyes of others too, whatever may be the ravages of time. In fact, perceptions of the evaluation of one's friends and the evaluation of one's husband correlate highly. Thus if one pictures one's husband as God-like, one remains convinced despite the passage of time that one is physically attractive. There are subtle issues of beauty and goodness and truth involved in these relationships (and they exist for men, too, though not so powerfully) and of how definitions of goodness and beauty and truth might change as one grows older. But given the right kind of husband (and to a lesser extent the right kind of wife), beauty need never fade, a spiritual truth of enormous importance, perhaps even more for the young than for the old.

The second question about the relationships among image of spouse, age and gender, is why the "U" curve relationship exists with age and why men are more likely to see their spouse as divine then women. The answer is that the three main variables in the model (CHARM, DISROBE, and NAKED) interact with age and gender in such a way that if these factors were equally distributed without regard to age and gender both the lines in the graph would be straight and the line for men and the line for women would merge.

Herein lies a complex "story" of man, woman,[7] and God with charm, delight, and vulnerability ebbing and flooding at different ages, a love story it would seem with a happy ending and perhaps the hint of an even happier one.

The point here is not that CHARM explains everything. Questions remain of why it is not evenly distributed and why, even if it were, it would still have differential impacts in various subpopulations. Yet it does seem to be the dominant variable in the analysis and to influence (or perhaps be influenced by) all the others. Nor is that fact so surprising. If the spouse is indeed mysterious, exciting, romantic, and a sharp dresser, one might well enjoy undressing for her and undressing her[8] and experience little shame or embarrassment over nakedness or sexual love. Such a lover might well seem divine.

In any case, there is surely room for improvement in CHARM among men: 63% of the men put their women above the mean on the CHARM scale, but only 40% of the women return the favor. Moreover, while it might be expected that when one desegregates the CHARM factor men would be more likely to describe their wives as sharper dressers than women would be to so describe their men (63% versus 35%). Men are also more likely to say their women are romantic (54% versus 42%), exciting (66% versus 53%), and mysterious (65% versus 54%). It should be noted finally that the CHARM scale does not correlate for either gender with the number of children still in the house; children therefore cannot be used as an excuse for either gender not to be CHARMing.

A Model from the "Song of Songs"?

One possible model for a quasi-divine spouse would look like this: A wife or a husband who is CHARMing creates an ambiance in the relationship in which embarrassment and prudery are diminished if not eliminated and the partners are free to revel in each other's naked bodies. The combination of charm and physical vulnerability creates the kind of (relatively) total openness and (relatively) complete vulnerability to the other that gives the other power over the self that seems akin to divine power, a power which is both overwhelming and delightful. This ambiance tends to be present at the beginning of a marriage but diminishes as the CHARM diminishes in the middle years. However, it recurs in the later years when the spouse becomes ever more delectable for those who see CHARM in the spouse. Indeed among those whose perception of CHARM in the spouse does not diminish, the quasi-divine image of the spouse does not decline either.

If this model is correct, the crucial elements in perceiving the spouse as a metaphor for God are the spouse's CHARM, one's own total and delightful physical vulnerability to the spouse, and the spouse's generous physical vulnerability to the self. One might then conclude that one strategy for the development of a spirituality of marriage would be emphasis on more CHARM (especially for men) and more delighted physical vulnerability.

This model would seem to come right out of the Song of Songs.

A metaphor is a two-way street, so much so that St. Paul in Ephesians becomes almost tongue-tied when he tries to talk about both poles of the metaphor at the same time. If the spouse is imagined to be like God because she or he is CHARMing (romantic, mysterious, exciting—and a sharp dresser[9]) and because he or she creates an atmosphere where bodily vulnerability is easy and delightful, the reason must be the respondent already has in his/her imagination an image of a CHARMing God with whom it is safe to trust even the most private and secret elements of one's being (and may not the whole of creation be imagined as God's "sharp" clothes?).

Such an image of God surely represents an experience of Grace, a hint of what God is like. Moreover, the experience is enhanced when that image is applied to the spouse. The self perceives the spouse as like God and God as like the spouse, and one's picture of both is sharpened and admiration for both heightened. One learns about the spouse from what one knows about God and about God from what one knows about the spouse. Moreover, such experiences of Grace seem to occur for approximately one out of every five married Americans. As far as I am aware no one has ever tried (save by a priori deductions) to discuss the actual Grace experiences of ordinary people and to isolate empirically the dynamics of such experiences.

Perhaps this metaphor of God and spouse occasions and is occasioned by a Grace experience which is commonplace and ordinary. It may not be at all like the mystical interludes described by Meister Eckhart or Teresa of Avila (though the latter did not hesitate to use sexual imagery) or William James. It may be unworthy of the notice of those who write ponderous volumes about spirituality. Nonetheless, since the Spirit blows whither She will, one must take Grace where one finds it.

And celebrate its appearance.

OBJECTIONS

Objections to this view will come from both the right and the left. On the left it will be argued that the experience of God as spouse and spouse as God cannot be considered politically or socially relevant. Humankind faces enormous problems—racial, gender and sexual chauvinism, poverty, hunger, environmental catastrophe. There can be no time for romance, for charm, for the absorption of man and woman in one another. Indeed, such ego-seeking love is almost surely politically incorrect because it is likely to interfere with and take time away from appropriate social commitments and agendas.

Human love may turn in on the ego (or the egos) but it need not do so. The relevant issue is whether the image of the divine spouse is necessarily selfish. There are at least some a priori reasons to believe that human love between man and woman can embrace the whole of humankind. To examine the possibility that this is possible, I turned to NORC's General Social Survey to see how the image of God as a Spouse instead of a Master effected attitudes on race and feminism. In fact, the more likely both men and women are to imagine God as a spouse the more likely are they to support feminism and to oppose racism. The "soft," and "romantic," and "gentle" metaphors are not incompatible with social concern. Quite the contrary they reinforce it. So it is not unlikely that those respondents in the *Faithful Attraction* study who think of the spouse as God (the opposite version of the metaphor) will also be more socially concerned.

The second objection will come from those on the right who will scoff that I cannot really be serious in my claim that a romantic spouse and mutual undressing are or can be a part of naming God. What does the body, especially two naked bodies playing with one another, have to do with God and the Spirit? Is this not the kind of shallow romanticism one would expect from a celibate cleric inexperienced in the real nature of marriage? Ought not the clergy and the Church, for reasons of modesty and appropriate thought and behavior, say nothing at all about nakedness? At least one prominent Catholic theologian would disagree:

> There is a deep connection between the mystery of creation, as a gift springing from love, and that beatifying "beginning" of the existence of man as male and female, in the whole truth of their body and their sex, which is the pure and simple truth of communion between persons . . . .

Precisely by traversing the depth of that original solitude, man now emerges in the dimension of the mutual gift, the expression of which—and for that very reason the expression of his existence as a person—is the human body in all the original truth of its masculinity and femininity.

The body . . . manifests the reciprocity and communion of persons. It expresses it by means of the gift as the fundamental characteristic of personal existence. This is the body: a witness to creation as a fundamental gift, and so a witness to Love as the source from which this same giving springs. Masculinity-femininity—namely, sex—is the original sign of a creative donation and of an awareness on the part of man, male-female, of a gift lived so to speak in an original way. Such is the meaning with which sex enters the theology of the body.

The theologian is John Paul II, and the quote is from his audience talk of January 9, 1980, "Nuptial Meaning of the Body."[10]

THE PRESENCE OF THE SPIRIT

In much of the popular and semipopular literature of liturgy and religious education, a rather dyspeptic view is taken of Americans. Such a view seems to favor a Church which has been purged of its materialist, secularist, individualist, consumerist members. Whether such a view of Americans is accurate or not (especially in comparison with citizens of other countries), whether such a purge would be possible (what if the targeted men and women refused to leave), and whether such exclusivism is compatible with the Catholic heritage are not the issues in the present context. Rather the issue is whether one can learn from them anything about the Name of God or whether they are such a dis-Spirited people that they are without religious experience and metaphors.

(An alternative position which I do not propose to argue here is that the Spirit is much more likely to flourish among the Catholic laity just now than She is among the hierarchy, the clergy, the theologians, the academics, the liturgists, and the religious educators because the laity do not put nearly so many obstacles in Her way as she blows whither She will. I often wonder whether She is altogether at ease, not being an academic, as She tries to sweep through the halls of divinity schools, seminaries, and theology departments—sociology departments, too, as far as that goes.)

I submit that the spousal image of God experienced by some of the laity described in the present chapter is a vivid and earthy challenge to the abstract and didactic God discourse of the professional theologians. The laity do have religious experiences after all, although they may not be the kind of experiences that theologians, liturgists, and religious educators would approve. God experienced in spousal nakedness?[11] How politically incorrect can you get?

Nonetheless, should theologians wish to learn more about the experience of God and the Names given to Him by the people of God, moderately ingenious survey research is one way to acquire such knowledge.

It may also be argued that the spousal metaphor as described in this essay is the name given to God by Americans. Men and women in other countries, especially third-world countries, may have no such experiences of either spouse or God. Nor for most of human history have such experiences been available. Against this position, however, one merely has to cite the Song of Songs or ancient Egyptian love poetry as proof that a CHARMing spouse, one that is exciting, mysterious, romantic, and elegant, a spouse before whom one delights in appearing naked while at the same time reveling in the beloved's nakedness, is an experience that is by no means limited to only one culture or time. The author of the Song apparently did not have God in mind (explicitly anyway). But it did not take long for commentators to see the metaphorical possibilities in her work. (Roland Murphy, O.Carm., has argued that the author of the Song may well be a woman.) Unfortunately, they usually weakened the human pole of the comparison and de-eroticized its meaning, a practice which the Christian churches have followed ever since, apparently for fear that the suggestion of a physical, sexually aroused human lover disclosing God would shock the ordinary people or perhaps make them enjoy sexual love "too much." Indeed, the Catholic Church, influenced by Augustine's sexual preoccupations, has done its best to pretend that marital sexual delight is almost totally unrelated to God's love for Her people, hardly a metaphor at all and barely a sacrament, to say nothing of a Sacrament.

CONCLUSION

The research reported in this chapter proves that the spousal metaphor is alive and well. One can, to paraphrase the proverb about sin, legislate against the romantic and erotic spousal metaphor for God, but one cannot make it unpopular.

God's real Name, David Tracy will argue, I believe, is Love. What kind of love? Doubtless many different kinds of love. But to exclude or minimize the spousal meaning of romantic and erotic love with the adored intimate other may be to deprive that Name of its richness and depth, of its power and origins, of its basic appeal and fundamental nature. The metaphor of God as lover is surely not fully disclosed in the marriage bed, but it begins there. Perhaps in some ways and for some spouses it ends there too—literally one step short of paradise in intense passion with the CHARMing and intimate other during the twilight years of life—a hint of love yet to come, a love(Love) that is as implacable as death, and even more so.

Fortunate spouses and, arguably, fortunate God to have so ingeniously revealed Himself.

Romantic Love: Ought the Faithful Be Consulted

Love, says the Brazilian proverb, is eternal, but it does not last. This wisdom, both traditional and conventional, seems at first obvious enough. Romantic love may be necessary for marriage to occur, but it surely is not necessary to sustain the marriage relationship which is based on more durable and less ephemeral qualities. Occasional bursts of romantic love may be useful, but they are not really required.

In the contemporary Catholic Church romantic love is not in good repute, it would seem. The right denounces it as ephemeral and, well, "romantic" and says pointedly that it is inappropriate for a priest to do such research.[1] The left complains that the research ignores the sexual politics of marriage and asserts that it is politically incorrect to study Eros in married heterosexuals.

Falling in love is a delicious experience, obsessing, delightful, exhausting, exhilarating, frustrating, wonderful, terrifying. Perhaps it is understandable that most men and women are relieved, if somewhat disillusioned, when it fades away. When one is in love, one is absorbed, preoccupied, tense and intense, and filled with a sexual longing which permeates the rest of existence, making it both glorious and exhausting. Wonderful as the interlude is, it is not clear that a whole life in love would be tolerable.

Yet is the question of romantic love finally settled? May it not provide challenges to Church teachers, to theologians, and perhaps even to married people? Can romantic love last? Do some people live happily ever after? Is romantic love a subject about which the faithful ought to be consulted?

At the end of the third volume of his magisterial series, Marriage in the Catholic Church, Theodore Mackin, S.J. posed two "stories" about marriage. The first is told by a man "whose acquaintance with sexuality has been only in the confessional, listening to the guilty accounts of adultery, fornication, masturbation or fornication. (He) will be inclined to think of it as a mingled physical and emotional urgency that even Catholics who confess find great difficulty in controlling . . . . It may be reduced to sexuality's brute minimum, an imperious energy as destructive as it is life-giving." (*The Marital Sacrament*, page 667)

"But which is the truer story about sexuality, that one or the one told by deeply happy spouses who are in love and frequently love making? If the former is the truer, the truth of the fathers' and the scholastics' indictment follows inescapably. The best that can be expected even among devout spouses is that it will produce children and stay with the marriage."[2]

If the latter story, that of the spouses who are in love, is truer, theology then is moving into the territory "barely explored by theologians and not at all by the Catholic authorities," the territory of Eros, the territory of the Song of Solomon, the territory of the happily married laity.[3]

In Mackin's own outline of a theory, "sin in the world at its core" is the fear of the loss of self; and Christ's redemptive work is to take away the fear of loss. "Who else but men and women who have risked their passion in marriage, who have tried to take down the protective barriers in their own souls and in their spouses' can say what sexual love may do to take away fear of the loss of privacy, of freedom, of self regard, even fear of the loss of the one chance for happiness in human love."[4]

Neither the theological community nor the teaching authority would deny that the lay experience of marriage should be listened to; as I noted in an earlier chapter, the present Pope has said that married people have a unique and indispensable contribution to make in the Church's understanding of sexuality. Nevertheless, neither has expended much effort on learning from the laity the religious meaning of their married sexuality. The Teaching Authority is content to consult with those whom it knows will echo what the Authority has already said. Theologians reflect on the experience of their friends and, if they are married, on their own experience. No one as far as I know has attempted to reflect on the experience of married men and women as captured in probability surveys.

Everyone uses "surveys" when generalizing about human behavior. Both the Teaching Authority and the theological community observe human behavior in a sample of people and generalize from that sample. They differ from the professional social scientist only in the size and randomness of the samples and the precision of the questions asked. I also note that, as Cardinal Martini has remarked somewhere, the "Sense of the Faithful" cannot be learned merely from social surveys but cannot be learned without them. I finally note that the Pope has remarked that the survey is one way of consulting with the faithful but not the only way.

Mackin's book is preoccupied necessarily with the issue of indissolubility: he is clearly uneasy with the notion that while the Church says in canon law that marriage is indissoluble, it in fact attributes sacramental indissolubility only to marriages between baptized Christians after their first act of sexual intercourse (assuming that both spouses possess the psychological maturity which would make subsequent annulment possible). Can a single act of intercourse, he wonders in effect, accomplish all that much?

I propose as an alternative and complementary model for investigating the nature of marriage to search for a group who have achieved empirical indissolubility—a group of humans most of whom believe that their marriage will never end in divorce.

The group I have selected are those who say that they are in the "falling in love" phase of the marriage cycle, 93% of whom say that divorce is for them impossible (as opposed to 72% of the rest of the population). I intend to ask what is the nature of this "falling in love" phase which so strongly implies that the marriage has become permanently indissoluble.[5]

It certainly seems to fade away quickly. In my survey (1450 married men and women, national probability sample) 47% of those in first year of marriage said they were in the falling-in-love phase, 35% in the second year, and 13% in the third year. Two years of romance seems to be the ration for most marriages.

Nonetheless, 17% of the respondents in the survey said that they were in the falling-in-love phase, while 65% said they were "settling down," three percent "bottoming out," and 25% "beginning again." Moreover, the "falling in love" response does not correlate either with age or duration of marriage. Romantic love need not and in fact does not fade away for those who are in love after the second year of marriage. There is some cyclic movement in the falling-in-love phase; but 60% of those who are in love now said they were five years ago, 70% two years ago, and 83% expect to be in love five years from now.

(Since there is no statistical difference between Protestants and Catholics—with one important exception to which I will return—in the proportion saying that they are "falling in love," my numbers are for the entire population and not just Catholics.)

Those in the falling-in-love phase are remarkably satisfied with their marriages. Ninety percent of them say that the spouse is their best friend (as opposed to 72% of the rest of the population). Ninety-six percent would marry the same person again (versus 79%). Eighty-one percent say that they are very happy in their marriage (as against 57%). The romantic lovers are certainly absorbed with one another—in fact 60% say that they are absorbed as opposed to 30% of the rest of the population. Seventy-four percent report sex more than once a week, and 54% say that there is a very great deal of satisfaction in their sexual life (31%). Thirty-two percent make love outdoors (22%); 28% swim in the nude (19%); 18% engage in prolonged sexual play a lot (11%); 28% engage in mutual undressing (9%); 40% enjoy stripping for their spouse (20%); 57% take showers or baths together (38%).

Feeling that you're in love with your spouse correlates with (and probably is both a cause of and an effect on) a very different kind of sexual and interpersonal life than that reported by other Americans. Those who are falling in love seem truly to be by love possessed.

The eyes of romantic love see the spouse in a different light than do the eyes of those not in that phase of the cycle. Eighty-eight percent say the spouse is exciting (versus 53%); 91% (versus 74%) say the spouse is kind. Seventy-four percent say the spouse is playful (versus 44%); 78% report that the spouse is romantic (versus 47%). Thirty-one percent say the spouse is mysterious and intriguing (as opposed to 16%). Forty-seven percent report that the spouse is God-like[6] (versus 24%).

"Romance" seems to result from a combination of religious and erotic behaviors which do not substitute for one another. Religious imagery, symbolism, and behavior are intimately connected to romance: half of those who think the spouse is God-like and who make love frequently (several times a week) say that they are falling in love as do only a fifth of those who make love frequently and do not see the spouse as god-like. The greatest payoff in romance, in other words, comes from (or relates to) a mix of religion or religious images and frequent sex.

The interaction between the religious and the erotic is intricate: both add independent explanatory power. Thus for example, when one cross-tabulates romance by joint showers and joint prayers, one finds that 9% of those who do neither are in the romantic phrase, 20% of those who do one or the other are in that phase, as are 30% of those who do both.

Intimate play actually increases with age for those who are in love. They start out in the early years of marriage less likely than those not in love to engage in prolonged intimate play, but the lines cross in the early thirties and play diminishes for those who are not in love and increases for those who are, so that after sixty-five those who are in love are four times as likely to report frequent and prolonged intimate play (20% versus 5%).

While the proportion who think the spouse is attractive diminishes with age for those who are not in love, it increases with age for those who are—so that nine out of ten of those who are in love over sixty-five insist that their spouse is attractive. All the more reason, it would seem, to undress him or her, the rate of which activity remains constant at 40% through the whole life cycle for those who are in love but falls from 30% to 10% for those who are not. Similarly, removing one's clothes to tease and delight the spouse is not a pastime which declines among those in love: two-fifths of them report such activity through the life cycle, while the rate declines from 30% to 10% for those not in love.

Those who are in love are also constant in their conviction that the spouse is a skilled lover—seven out of every ten of them believe this no matter how old they might be, while the rate declines to four out of ten for those who are not in love. The image of the self as a skillful lover increases with age for those in love. At the early ages of life, only about a fifth of the respondents considered themselves skilled lovers. For those who are not in love that rate does not change. For those who are, the rate more than doubles during the life cycle so that almost five out of ten of the romantic lovers over sixty-five say that they are skilled lovers.

The abandonment of all sexual inhibitions in married love, perhaps a operational indicator of Father Mackin's reference to taking "down the protective barriers in their own souls and their spouses," does not happen at all in half of American marriages, but it does occur in three-fifths of the marriages in which the respondents say they are falling in love.[7]

The image of God has an important influence on romantic love. Those who see God as a lover, a spouse, a friend, and a mother are twice as likely to say they are in the falling-in-love phase than those who see God as a judge, master, king, and father. St. Paul was right: the two loves, human and divine, do correlate one with another.

Finally, the twenty-two percentage point advantage those who are in the romantic love stage of the marriage cycle have over others in empirical indissolubility can be reduced to statistical insignificance if one takes into account joint prayer, frequent prolonged sexual play, the skill of the spouse as a lover, and the quality of sexual fulfillment in the relationship. Prayer accounts for about half of the difference explained. The sexual variables account for the other half. Thus romantic love makes divorce less likely precisely because those who perceive themselves to be in love are more likely to pray together and more likely to enjoy an intense erotic life. Praying together and playing together does indeed account for husband and wife being more likely to stay together.

None of this, however, shows a distinctive Catholic experience of falling in love, does it? Catholics are not any more likely to say that they are in this phase of the marriage cycle, save under one condition: they also say that they imagine their spouse as like a God. For both Catholics and Protestants, there is a statistically significant correlation between picturing the spouse as like a God; but the correlation for Catholics is three times as high: .35 versus .12. In terms of variance explained, a "divine" spouse accounts for 12% of the variance in falling in love for Catholics and 1% of the variance for Protestants. Figure 1 demonstrates the interaction between Catholicism and religious imagery on marital sex that we have come to expect. Sacramental imagery has a far more powerful impact for Catholics than for others.

Here is proof of a distinctive Catholic imagination and proof, if I may say so, with a vengeance. The image one has of God as a lover is far more likely to drive one into the giddiness of romantic love if one is Catholic then if one is Protestant.

Catholics then should beware of thinking their husband or wife is quasi-divine, and especially of saying that the metaphor "strongly applies." If they do endorse the metaphor, then they are likely to be trapped, perhaps permanently, in the volatile, dizzy, alluring, sexually hungry miasma of romantic love.

Poor People, Huh!

The very mention of the statistics cited in the previous paragraphs seems to offend many people. Married lovers ought not to answer questions about their erotic playfulness (though in my survey they did not seem reluctant to do so). Or if they do talk about it, what they say ought not to be recorded or it ought not to be published, "surely not in a Catholic publication." One ought not to correlate nakedness (in a shower or bath) with prayer; it is almost sacrilegious. Certainly one ought not to say that a judicious mixture of prayer and sexual play produces empirical indissolubility. These objections which I hear from both the left and the right (in slightly different forms) raise the question of whether my research is prurient or the reaction is prudish. In a day when some liberal theologians want to include homosexual unions in the norm for human intimacy and conservative hierarchies are obsessed with the mechanics of the pro-creative process, it is hilarious to suggest that interest in the correlates of romantic love is prurient.

Do the data in my study present a picture of how man and woman ought to relate to one another throughout the course of their marriage? Is it for this kind of intimacy that the species was designed by whatever or Whoever was responsible for the design? The data show only that for some people such a life is possible. Data do not impose obligations. However, data may open up possibilities both for married lovers and for reflecting theologians and official teachers..

Romantic love persists among some married men and women because of (or in relationship to) a complicated interaction of chemistry, history, psychology, sensitivity, and religion. The romantic marriage is not a typical marriage. In fact, it probably represents a form of marital intimacy that most married people do not think possible or reject if they think it remotely possible. Life is too busy, too serious, too filled with responsibilities, to pursue hearts and flowers and lace except on Saint Valentine's day.

Yet romance as a sustained pattern of marital intimacy not only happens, it happens in about a sixth of the married population, and it tends to be remarkably durable. Moreover, it correlates with an extraordinary life of sexual activity and playfulness as well as of religious devotion and excludes almost completely the perceived possibility of divorce.

It is difficult if not impossible to sort out the natural history of such a sustained love affair without detailed information which follows such couples through a long period of their relationship. How the various dynamics which are at work interact as mutual cause and effect is something about which we can in the present state of our knowledge only speculate. We do not know yet how such love affairs are launched, how they are sustained, and how they survive. But we do know that romantic lovers are deliriously content with their spouses whose admirable characteristics they praise in overwhelming numbers.

To turn to questions for the theologians and Church Teaching Authority:

1. Might not the romantic love depicted in the marriages of this one-sixth of the population be the metaphor par excellence for the love of God for His people and Jesus for His Church? The metaphor will exist in other marriages, of course, but not in such an intense fashion and hence not be so excellent a self-disclosure of God.

2. Might not Eros, as Father Mackin suggests, and erotic playfulness be an ultimate empirical correlate of indissolubility and hence a goal to be urged by religious teachers and authorities? Could it not be said, to expand Father Peyton's famous dictum, that the husband and wife who tend to pray together and to play together erotically (not necessarily both behaviors at the same time) also tend to stay together?

3. Might not the abandon of sexual inhibitions, as Father Mackin implies, be one indicator (not the only one) of the disappearance of the protective barriers which represent sin in the world? As such, might not the goodness of such abandon be an appropriate matter for theological reflection and Christian education?

4. Does not the relationship between erotic play and religious imagery and devotion suggest that the biblical metaphor in which sexual love is taken to be a hint of divine love deserves to be taken more seriously and more concretely than most theologians and Teaching Authority pronouncements have thus far been willing to admit? Might not the Song of Songs, after all, be paradigmatic?

5. Should not theologians and teachers both reconsider their skepticism about romantic love and reflect on it as sacramental and indeed as Sacramental?

6. Should not then the experience of romance and abandon in married love become a (not the) primary source of theological reflection both about marriage and sexuality?

These seem to me to be, in light of the facts, perfectly reasonable questions. Yet whenever I discuss this subject, I am met with giggles from academics and fury from non-academics. Some people storm out of the room, others sneer and ridicule. A colleague remarked that she would not want to know men and women so absorbed with one another because they would be dull. A woman in the audience at a lecture told me that the questions asked were none of anyone's business and that people would lie in response to them.

After a skeptical, not to say hostile, press conference, a woman reporter explained in a whisper, "that's the kind of marriage we all want, we're disappointed because we don't have it, and we're afraid to try it."

I think that is what Father Mackin called "sin in the world at its core."

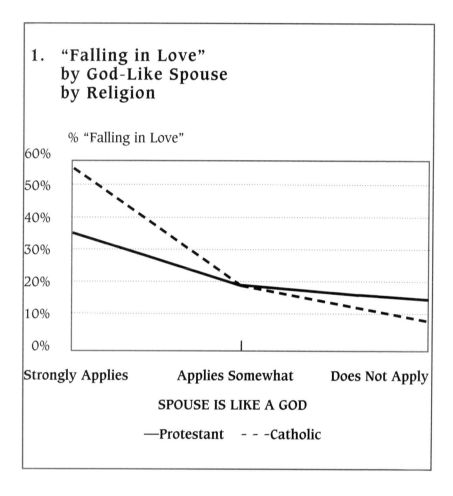

1. "Falling in Love"
   by God-Like Spouse
   by Religion

% "Falling in Love"

60%
50%
40%
30%
20%
10%
0%

Strongly Applies   Applies Somewhat   Does Not Apply

SPOUSE IS LIKE A GOD

——Protestant   - - -Catholic

Sex and Religion in Young Marriages

In the late 1970s, under a grant from the Knights of Columbus, NORC undertook a study of young Catholics between the ages of fifteen and thirty.[1] When a respondent was married, a questionnaire was also administered to the respondent's spouse. Thus it was possible to examine not only one person's view of a marriage relationship but also the joint view of husband and wife. Moreover, since the sample was large there were three hundred and thirty-seven *families* (husband and wife) which we were able to analyze. Finally, there was room in the questionnaire for more detailed questions about both religion and marital relationships than could be placed in the ordinary General Social Survey questionnaire. While the theory of religion as poetry was not so well developed at that time and the measurements of religious imagery not yet as simple as they would become when they were introduced into the General Social Survey in 1983, the findings from the Young Catholic study are still useful for enriching our understanding of the Catholic experience of sex. There is unfortunately no comparison group of young people who are not Catholic, but since I have already established in earlier chapters that there is something a little different about the Catholic experience of sex, this chapter will serve to explain in part how this different experience gets transmitted from generation to generation and how husbands and wives reinforce it in one another.

One of the most interesting findings of the study was what I called the *Kramer vs. Kramer* finding (based on a movie popular at that time about the breakup of a young marriage): marital satisfaction and sexual fulfillment are high in the first two years of marriage and then diminish sharply till the end of the seventh year of marriage. After the eighth year there is a substantial rebound.[2] The question then becomes whether the rebound in marital satisfaction and sexual fulfillment is in part at least a rebound of warm religious images. If it is, then we have yet more proof that the Catholic experience of marital sex is unique.

My theory leads to the following expectations:

1. Family experience in childhood will affect the religious images of an adult and through that imagery marital happiness. The warmer the childhood, the "warmer" the religious imagery.

2. Warm religious imagery will, in turn, affect both the capacity to express love and the capacity for sexual fulfillment. The warmer the religious imagery of husband and wife (as expressed in a joint measure), the more likely they will both be to describe a "warm" (i.e., "excellent") situation in their family with regard to both sexual fulfillment and capacity for loving.

3. In turn, marital satisfaction (both "very satisfied") will be to a considerable extent shaped by "warm" religious imagery and "warm" sexual fulfillment.

4. As a marriage develops, there will be stronger correlations between the wife's religious imagery and the husband's religious imagery.

5. Much of the decline in sexual fulfillment and its subsequent rise will be explainable by a model

which takes into account family "warmth,"
religious "warmth," and the perceived capacity
to love.

6. Much of the decline in marital satisfaction and
its subsequent rise will be explainable by a
model which takes into account family
"warmth," religious "warmth," the perceived
capacity to love, and sexual fulfillment.

7. Religious warmth and sexual fulfillment will be
the critical variables in the rebound of
marriages at the end of their first decade.

8. Those who have intense religious experiences
will have warmer religious imagery and hence
more satisfying marriages.

Sex, Religion, and Marital Happiness

I selected as measures of "warm" religious imagery — God as
a lover, Jesus as warm, Mary as warm, and the afterlife as a
"paradise of pleasure and delight." (Each of these images,
incidentally, is a story because it implies an ongoing relationship.) I constructed a five-point scale from these items to
measure the relationship between individual (as opposed to
joint husband-wife) religious imagery and marital adjustment. The relationship is quite powerful. Thirty-three percent
of those who thought of none of the warm images as
"extremely likely" reported excellent sexual fulfillment in
marriage, as opposed to 69% of those who checked all four as
"extremely likely." Similarly, 27% of those low on the scale
described the value consensus in their marriage as excellent,
as opposed to 63% of those who are high on the scale.
Religious images, then, do indeed affect the quality of married
life as that quality is perceived by an individual respondent.
But my concern in this chapter is, rather, the combined
imagery of husband and wife and how that affects their
combined view of their marital satisfaction.

I used factor analysis to create a "joint religious image scale" which included the images of both respondent and spouse. It correlated positively and significantly with marital satisfaction, sexual fulfillment, and value consensus. If there is an atmosphere in the marriage in which husband and wife tend to share warm religious imagery, then their marriage satisfaction, their sexual fulfillment, and their value consensus are likely to be higher than if they do not share such religious imagery. How you imagine Jesus, God, Mary and the afterlife does, indeed, affect your marital satisfaction and your sexual fulfillment. Religious images do have an impact on what goes on in the bedroom (although, of course, people need not be aware of this impact).

If husband and wife are on the high end of the religious warmth scale, they are 16 percentage points more likely to say that they are both very satisfied with the marriage, 14 percentage points more likely to both say that their sexual adjustment is excellent, and 12 percentage points more likely to say that their value consensus is excellent. All three differences are statistically significant.

Religious warmth, in other words, is good for a marriage. Religious warmth and marital warmth correlate with one another. Religious warmth declines in the middle years of the first decade of marriage, at the time spouses are experiencing an increase in problems in their marriage life and individual respondents are experiencing problems in their religious belief systems. However, in the last two years of the marriage the warmth scale seems to rebound to where it was at the beginning of the marriage. Furthermore, as hypothesized in proposition four at the beginning of this chapter, there is much greater convergence between husband and wife in their religious imagery as the story of their marriage develops. In the last two years of the first decade of marriage, there are strong and statistically significant correlations between husbands and wives in their view of God as a lover (.40) and in their view of afterlife as a paradise of pleasure and delight (.23). Common religious imagery, then, does indeed tend to emerge out of the "story" of a common life together.

The story of this convergence is dramatically illustrated by this finding: In the first two years of marriage it is likely that if your spouse says that God is a lover, you will think so, too. This proportion declines precipitously from 79% to 51% by the middle of the marriage. In other words, at that time, your spouse's influence on imagery (and vice versa) has practically fallen by twenty-eight percentage points. But in the final two years of the first decade of marriage, the convergence becomes quite dramatic again. Your spouse's image of God has a far more powerful impact on you than it has had since the first year of the marriage. On the other hand, if your spouse is not likely to think of God as a lover, the deterioration of your own image of God as a lover continues even into the ninth and the tenth year of the marriage. The greatest difference between those whose spouse says it is extremely likely that God is a lover and those whose spouse does not say so is in the final two years of the decade. Sixty-seven percent of those whose spouse says it is "extremely likely" that God is a lover say themselves that it is "extremely likely"; whereas only 12% of those whose spouse says it is not likely that God is a lover say themselves that it is likely for them to think of God as a lover. In other words, by the end of the first decade of marriage if your spouse thinks of God as a lover, it is highly probable that you will. If your spouse does not think that way, it is very improbable that you will think of God as a lover.

Furthermore, sexual fulfillment in marriage has a considerable impact on the image of God as a lover. Seventy-one percent of those who say that their sex life together is excellent say that God is a lover and their spouse says that God is a lover. Only 56% of those with less than excellent sexual adjustment reflect the spouse's conviction that God is a lover. Precisely then, in those marriages where the sexual fulfillment is high, there is the strongest relationship between a spouse's image of God as a lover and one's own image of God as a lover.

Nineteen percent of our respondents are likely to imagine God as a mother. Twenty-eight percent of those who have spouses who think of God as a mother share this imagination, whereas only 17% of those whose spouses do not think of God as a mother have this imagination themselves. The convergence of imagery of God as mother increases as the years of marriage increase. The size of the correlation between the spouses' image of God as mother doubles between the third year and the eighth year of marriage. Finally, the association between spouses on the subject of the maternity of God is much stronger in marriages in which the spouses are very satisfied (gamma = .37) than it is in marriages where both spouses are not very satisfied (gamma = .16). Thus, both marital satisfaction and the passage of time leads to a convergence, even of the somewhat unusual image of the maternity of God.

Thus "warm" religious imagery raises the marital satisfaction and sexual fulfillment, and husband-wife imagery converges after the mid-decade marital crisis, as a common marriage "story" evolves and a common repertoire of religious imagery tends to appear to resonate with the story, both influencing it and being influenced by it.

I have established, then, that religious imagery affects both sexual fulfillment and marital satisfaction. I now must turn to the question of whether warmth of past family life also relates to present marital warmth. There are statistically significant, though moderate, relationships between a respondent's description of happiness as a child and joint satisfaction with a marriage, joint sexual fulfillment in a marriage, and value consensus in a marriage. There are also statistically significant relationships between closeness to the mother and joint satisfaction and value consensus, and between closeness to the father and sexual fulfillment. Happy and intimate childhoods, in other words, relate positively though modestly with happy marriages.

Furthermore, and finally, adult religious imagery is related modestly but significantly to childhood experiences both of the respondent and the respondent's spouse. Warm religious imagery acts as a "funnel" which gathers together childhood influences and passes them on to marital evaluation. The joint religious imagery scale correlates significantly (at a level in excess of .2) both with "excellent" sexual fulfillment as reported by both spouses and "excellent" capacity to express love and affection as reported by both spouses. The love and affection capacity does not directly relate to marital satisfaction but influences marital satisfaction through its connection with sexual fulfillment. To wrap up the package: marital satisfaction is influenced by sexual fulfillment; sexual fulfillment is influenced by warm religious imagery; and warm religious imagery is influenced by childhood experiences. The religious "stories" about a person's life (as in religious imagery) act as a link between childhood family experiences and adult family experiences. The links are modest, I have said, because there are many other factors which impinge on the development of religious imagery, sexual fulfillment, and marital satisfaction. Nevertheless, religious images do precisely what our theory suggests they would do: they are the "stories" which link the beginning of the story of a person's life in his/her family of orientation with the middle of his/her story in the family of procreation and point towards the ending of the story—an ending, if the warm religious imagery is to be believed, which will involve a love affair in a paradise of pleasure and delight. Even if the imagery is wrong, it still makes for happier marriages (and one will leave to the philosophers and theologians whether such a pragmatic conclusion is evidence for truthfulness of the stories contained in the religious imagery).

I have noted that the path of decline and rebirth of marital happiness is paralleled by a decline and rebirth in religious attitudes, images, and behaviors. I now must draw this analysis towards a conclusion and ask whether one decline can account for the other.

This question can be answered by using a technique of multiple regression analysis called "residual" analysis. It is sufficient to say that one endeavors to diminish percentage point differences by taking into account the influence of variables which are hypothesized as being accountable for the difference. Thus, for example, one finds fifty percentage points difference between Irish Catholics and Jews in the amount of alcohol consumed at a given sitting, and one hypothesizes that this difference can be explained in part by parental drinking behavior. If when the mother's drinking behavior is put into the regression equation the residual percentage diminishes from 50 to 30, then one can say that two-fifths of the difference between Irish Catholics and Jews in drinking is accounted for by the fact that Irish mothers drink more than Jewish mothers. If another ten percentage point decrease occurs when the father's influence is included in the regression equation, then one can say that the joint influence of mother and father diminishes the difference by thirty percentage points and thus "explains" three-fifths of the difference between the Irish and the Jewish in drinking and leaves two-fifths difference unexplained by a model which takes into account *only* maternal and paternal drinking.

I used a similar technique to account for the decline of thirteen percentage points in the joint agreement by spouses that their sexual fulfillment is "excellent" between the first two years of marriage and the middle years of marriage. The difference declines by three percentage points when one takes into account childhood relationships. Since childhood relationships have long since been accomplished, one suspects that this results from a reconsideration and a reevaluation of the childhood experience. A much greater explanatory power is added to the model when religious imagery is taken into account. The difference is diminished to seven percentage points, and half of the decline in sexual fulfillment has been accounted for by a combination of warm religious imagery and childhood experience. Since the childhood experience is all reflected through religious imagery, one can say that about one-half of the decline in sexual fulfillment in young Catholic marriages can be attributable to the decline in the middle years of the marriage of their warm religious intimacy. Finally, when the ability of both spouses to express love and affection is taken into account, the difference is reduced by two percentage points, and almost two-thirds of the decline in sexual fulfillment in the young Catholic marriage has been accounted for.

Precisely the same pattern may be observed in explaining the increase in sexual fulfillment between the middle years and the ninth and tenth years of the marriage. In this critical turning point, the level of sexual satisfaction goes up twenty-one percentage points, and more than three-fifths of that increase can be accounted for by family experience and warm religious imagery (the latter of which is indeed the funnel for childhood experiences).

In the process of working out the sexual problems in the middle years of the first decade of marriage, Catholic spouses—in all likelihood, quite un-self-consciously—are powerfully influenced by a dramatic resurgence in the climate of warm religious imagery in their new family. The increase in sexual fulfillment is sacramental and revelatory and gives the couple greater confidence in the loving warmth of God. On the other hand, the loving warmth of God seems also to give them greater confidence, to strive for stronger, better sexual intimacy.

The same four variable models (adding sexual fulfillment to ability to express love and affection, religious imagery, and childhood experiences) can be applied to the decline and resurgence of marital satisfaction. Marital satisfaction declines from the first to the eighth year of marriage by some nineteen percentage points. Most of the explanatory power of the model is contributed by the decline in warm religious imagery and by the decline in the capacity to express love and affection; together with childhood experiences these variables explain two-thirds of the decline, and sexual fulfillment, as such, when added to the model, attributes no further explanatory power. However, both the ability to express love and affection and religious imagery and childhood experience are funneled through sexual fulfillment. The decline in sexual fulfillment is not the "cause" of the decline in marital satisfaction, it is the conduit through which these prior causes work.

The same model explains 55% of the twenty percentage point increase in marital satisfaction from the eighth to the tenth year of marriage. Again, the principal explanatory variables in the resurgence of marital satisfaction are the increase in the warmth of religious imagery and the increase in confidence of one's ability to express love and affection. These factors, plus the childhood experience variable, are channeled to marital satisfaction through their impact on sexual fulfillment.

Religious imagery, then, plays an extraordinarily important part in the decline and rebirth of marital happiness, it directly influences and channels childhood experiences toward decline and rebirth of sexual fulfillment in marriage, and it, in turn, operates through its impact on the ability to love and sexual fulfillment on marital satisfaction in the Catholic family. To summarize the model: warm families of origin produce warm religious imagery which in turn produces warm sexuality which in turn produces warm marriages. The decline of religious imagery and the decline of sexual fulfill-ment account for most of the decline in general marital satisfaction, and also, the rebirth of religious warmth, sexual warmth, and love warmth leads at the end of the first decade of marriage to a rebirth of marital satisfaction.

To test the eighth hypothesis presented at the beginning of this chapter, 64% of those who have had intense religious experiences often or sometimes describe their sexual fulfillment as excellent as opposed to 43% who have had hese experiences rarely or never—a statistically significant difference. Furthermore, those who have had religious experiences are twenty percentage points more likely to think of God as a lover (an interesting result of having been in the presence of an "overwhelming power which seemed to lift you out of yourself"). The question then arises as to whether it is precisely among those ecstatics who xperience God as a lover that there is the greatest likelihood of reporting excellent sexual fulfillment in marriage. Indeed it is, precisely among those who both think of God as lover and who have had religious experiences often or sometimes.

Sixty-nine percent of those who have had religious experiences and think of God as lover report their sexual fulfillment as "excellent" as opposed to 48% of those who have had similar experiences and do not think of God as lover. Religious experience, in other words, helps your sexual fulfillment only if it makes you more likely to think of God as lover.

RELIGIOUS LIFE CYCLE, MARRIAGE, AND RELIGIOUS IMAGERY

Young Catholics, like members of other religious traditions, go through a "U" curve in religious practice from the late teens to the twenties, a decline which reaches its nadir in the middle twenties and then rebounds sharply—though not to previous levels—in the late twenties. This age cycle of religious devotion seems to so closely parallel the cycle of marital satisfaction described previously that it seems safe to assume as a working hypothesis that the two phenomena are related if not identical. In my attempt to explain the religious life cycle, then, I propose the following specific hypotheses:

1. Decline of religious devotion of American Catholics is a form of partial withdrawal of affiliation or "alienation" from the institutional Church which parallels a withdrawal from other institutions in society.

2. Given the enormous disagreement between the attitudes on sexual matters of young Catholics and the teachings of the institutional Church, it is hypothesized that a strong contributor to the institutional disaffiliation will be the attitudes of young Catholics on premarital sex and on living together before marriage.

3. Given what we have seen in the previous chapters about the relationship between marriage and religious devotion, it is hypothesized that a

substantial part of the rebound phenomenon will be explainable in terms of marriage reintegrating young people into social institutions, and in particular into the Church. A marriage between two Catholics, and especially a marriage to a devout spouse, will facilitate this reintegration.

4. "Warm" religious imagery will, in part, cancel the effect of attitudes of sexual permissiveness, and the increase of shared warm religious imagery in a marriage will reduce even more the effect of attitudes of sexual permissiveness.

The last point is worth dwelling on because it is a theoretical proposition derived from the perspective on religion laid out previously: warm images of God combined with, reinforced by, and reinforcing a warm marital relationship will tend to reduce the effect of attitudes supportive of sexual promiscuity and sexual intimacy without public commitment.

Note well that the expectation described in the previous paragraph runs strongly against the conventional wisdom. First of all, it would seem unlikely that a young person's images of God and of Mary and of the afterlife would have much, if any, effect on her/his approach to premarital sex; not in a "pagan," "hedonistic," and secularist society like our own. Secondly, if one were to expect any influence at all, one might well think it reasonable that someone who believes that God is a lover and that heaven is a paradise of pleasure and delight would also think that there is nothing wrong with the delightful pleasures of love in this life being enjoyed whenever and wherever possible. That warm religious imagery, in other words, which previously was demonstrated to promote sexual fulfillment in marriage would also reasonably be expected to promote sexual freedom before marriage.

Nonetheless, I am hypothesizing the opposite phenomena. "Stories" implicit in the "warm" religious images are stories of fidelity, commitment, of promises made, honored, and kept permanently. I therefore predict a negative correlation between warm images and attitudes of sexual permissiveness—even though such a prediction may seem to some readers to be absurd. At least, unlike other pontifications about youthful sex, mine can be tested immediately.

In the United States, there was in the late 1970s a sharp decline with age in religious devotion (as measured by a scale composed of prayer, mass attendance, and the reception of communion). Sixty-four percent of those between fourteen and eighteen are high on this scale, while those in their later twenties (between 26 and 28) only place 22% high on that scale. There is a modest rebound of religious activity in the late twenties; from 22% to 29%. The religious revival which seems to occur at the end of the decade of the twenties (bringing young people back to approximately the level of religious devotion in their early twenties) represents a significant upward change of young Catholic religious behavior.[3] The cycle applies to both men and women. Women are more devout than men, and their cycle is approximately ten percentage points higher than that of the men, starting out at 69%, declining at 27%, and rebounding to 34%; while men begin at 60%, decline to 17%, and bounce back to 22%.

I suspected that the decline could be explained by spouse's religion (if the respondent was married), whether indeed one was married, alienation from the religious institution, and attitudes towards sexual permissiveness. The model I postulated explained a quarter of the variance in religious behavior. Marriage in the United States seems to produce a higher level of opposition to sexual permissiveness and a greater degree of confidence in the organizational and institutional structures of the society. Young people go through a dramatic period of alienation in their twenties, turning off all social institutions including the Church. However, when they "settle down" and begin a family of their own, they become both more hostile of permissiveness and more confident of the organizational structures of the society. Marriage, apparently, reintegrates them into the society and also into the Church—especially in the latter case if the spouse is Catholic.

So our hypothetical model does indeed explain a satisfactory amount of the variance in religious devotion. The question now becomes whether permissiveness and alienation change as young people grow older and whether this change can account for the change in their religious behavior. I now propose to use the same technique of "residual analysis" used previously to see if the variables in our model can account for much of the religious life cycle—both the decline from the early to the middle twenties and then the rise at the end of the late twenties. There is no rise at all in religious devotion at the end of the twenties for those who are not married. It would, therefore, appear that the rise in the religious devotion among young Catholics who are between twenty-nine and thirty years old is almost entirely a function of the fact that more at that age are likely to be married and that married peoples' religious devotion is higher than that of single people.

By merely taking into account marriage and the religiousness of spouse one can account for almost nine-tenths of the twenty-six percentage points difference on the religious devotion scale between those in their early twenties and those between twenty-six and twenty-eight. In other words, those in their early and middle twenties who are married do not experience the sharp decline in religious practice that singles experience, particularly if they are married to Catholics. Marriage, and especially a marriage to a Catholic, reintegrates them into the social structure of the country and into the organizational structure of the Church.

Similarly, almost nine-tenths of the rebound can be accounted for by factors related to marriage. The apparent religious life cycle is in fact part of a larger life cycle. Those who are married are more likely to be religious than those who are not, presumably because marriage, particularly to one of the same faith, puts higher value on social and institutional integration. Marriage, in other words, cancels the alienation that goes on among the "non-married." The dynamics of the religious life cycle are now clear. Religious behavior goes up in the late twenties because more people are married in their late twenties.

Not only are people in their late twenties more likely to be married, but those married people in their late twenties are also more likely to be devout. Among those between twenty-nine and thirty, 18% of the "non-marrieds" are high on the religious devotion scale, 20% of the Catholics in mixed marriages, and 46% of Catholics in Catholic marriages.

We have answered the question of why married people are more likely to be devout than single people: they are less alienated, though if they are in a religiously mixed marriage they are not much less alienated from the Church. Two remaining questions must be answered: what goes on in a Catholic marriage that leads to a resurgence of religious devotion and why do some Catholics choose to marry other Catholics and some choose to marry non-Catholics? Approximately one-half of the fifty-five percentage point difference in religious devotion between the two kinds of Catholic marriages can be accounted for by the model, and more than half of that half by the fact that in devout Catholic marriages the husband and wife share warm religious images. It is precisely the "stories of God" which husband and wife have worked out together that play a major share in explaining why they are devout and their counterparts who do not have these stories are not devout. The model is most successful in explaining the differences between the two kinds of Catholic marriages in the key age group of those between twenty-nine and thirty. More than three-fifths of the variance in the fifty-nine percentage point difference can be dealt with by our explanatory model. Furthermore, warm religious images also account for half of the differences in alienation from the Church between those who are high on the permissiveness scale and those who are low. Permissive young Catholics are sixteen percentage points more likely to be alienated from the Church than non-permissive, and this can be attributed to the fact that the non-permissive share warmer "stories of God."

The impact of images of God on devotion, permissiveness, and alienation can also be described in percentage form. Forty-five percent of those who have warm images are high on the religious devotion scale as opposed to 27% of those who do not have such images. The highest proportion of devout Catholics can be found among those who have both devout spouses and joint warm imagery—78% of those with devout spouses and warm imagery are themselves high on the religious devotion scale as opposed to 58% of those who have devout spouses but who lack warm "stories of God." It is a help, of course, if your spouse is devout, but the help is much greater (and "significantly" greater) if you also share common "warm religious imagery."

I hypothesized that warm religious images would have an effect on both permissive attitude and the feeling of alienation from the Church and, hence, would affect the levels of religious devotion in Catholic marriages. If a couple shares warm "stories of God," both will be more opposed to permissiveness, less alienated from the Church, and hence more devout. Religious imagery does indeed diminish both permissiveness and alienation. Those who have warm stories of God in their creative imagination are more opposed to premarital sex and living together than those who do not and are also likely to feel less alienated from the Church. In families where couples share these warm religious images, there will be less support for permissiveness, less feeling of alienation, and greater religious devotion.

I must now determine how these warm religious images work in Catholic marriages to "de-alienate" Catholic young people. First of all, high levels of religious practice in Catholic marriages are only to be found when both the respondent and the spouse are high on the religious devotion scale. There is virtually no difference between those in religiously mixed marriages and those who do not have a devout spouse with regard to their own religious devotion. Indeed, of the twenty-nine and thirty year level, those in mixed marriages seem more devout than those in Catholic marriages without a devout spouse. In those marriages where the spouse is devout, the respondent's level of religious devotion declines from 81% to 67% between the early and middle twenties but then bounces back to 72% in the late twenties. Can my analytic model explain some of the differences in religious devotion between those Catholics who have devout spouses and those who do not?

A third of those with warm images describe themselves as close to the Church, significantly different from one-fifth of those who do not have warm images. Furthermore, there is not a statistically significant difference in alienation between those who are more permissive and those who are less permissive if they have warm images. It is only among those who lack such images that the more permissive are statistically more likely to be alienated. Indeed, those who have high permissive attitudes and warm images are as likely to be close to the Church as those who have low permissive attitudes but lack the warm images. Imagery, in other words, seems to cancel out the relationship between permissive sexual attitudes and alienation from the Church. Warm religious images not only lead to a decrease in sexual permissiveness, but they also seem to eliminate the relationship between permissiveness and alienation.

Warm stories of God do not eliminate, by any means, the propensity of young people to be tolerant of sexual permissiveness (but they do diminish it substantially). Eighty-four percent of the people in marriages where the spouses do not have a common warm story of God are high on the permissive scale as opposed to 57% of those whose family has developed a mutual warm religious imagery. Forty-three percent of those with warm images think that living together is wrong as opposed to 17% who lack such images. However, there is virtually no difference between the two groups in their attitudes on birth control.

The stories of God that a husband and wife share, then, play an important part in the modest religious revival which occurs at the end of the late twenties, especially because these images have a notable impact on that group from which the revivalists are most likely to come—marriages in which both partners are Catholic.

Therefore, marriage adjustment and religious life cycle are both powerfully and importantly affected by a person's religious images, and in particular by the joint religious images that a husband and wife share. They do not explain the whole of marital satisfaction or the whole of the religious revival which seems to occur the late twenties. No one could reasonably expect that they would, for human behavior, particularly behavior as complex as religious devotion and marital relationships, is affected by a variety of biological, cultural, educational, biographical, and psychological factors—as well as, of course, by free human choice. Still, religious imagery plays a role, an important role, and indeed, in the religious revival at the end of the twenties, a *very* important role, articularly the common religious imagery that a husband and wife share.

There is a complex, intricate process by which husbands and wives work out, perhaps implicitly, a common religious posture in the first decade of their marriage. The posture is affected by their past experiences and affects many of their present attitudes and behaviors and will, doubtless, shape their future. It is the formation of a family religious "stance" that is intimately affected by and intimately affects the general satisfaction of their relationship, even though they themselves do not seem to perceive this because the process is so subtle and complex. In this chapter I have been able to describe some of the dynamics which seem to be at work, dynamics which may seem to many readers to be very intricate and complex. In fact, my models are much too simple, and the reality of husband/wife interactions as they resolve their problems and fashion a religious story which is no longer "yours and mine" but "ours" is infinitely more complex than the models I have laid out.

HUMAN INTIMACY AND DIVINE INTIMACY: AN EMPIRICAL TEST

Christian religious theory has always maintained that there is a link between human love and divine love. Marriage is, according to St. Paul, a "great sacrament," that is to say, a "revelation" of God's love for His people. As husband and wife love one another, so do God and the Church. Similarly, husband and wife ought in their relationship to try to imitate the love of God for the Church. The imagery is a two-way street: marriage revealing the passion of God's love for His people, and the generosity of God's love providing an ideal for the married life. St. Paul himself frequently gets his syntax confused as he tries to go in opposite directions on the symbolic street.

In traditional Christian marriage catechesis, much has been made of the relationship between "the two loves." If human spouses love God strongly, it is argued, they will also love one another strongly. Their faith in God will strengthen their faith in one another, and their love for one another will motivate them to grow in love of God.

It is often hard to tell how serious this catechesis is taken. Does the overarching "story" of God's love affect the emerging "story" of "our love," and does "our" love, one for another, rebound back to intensify our involvement in God's story?

Does divine intimacy really affect human intimacy and vice versa? How closely are the two love stories related? Is the relationship merely a matter of conventional piety without any measurable impact on people's lives? Or is it a fair measure of intimacy with God and sexual love?

If one takes prayer as an image of intimacy with God and sexual fulfillment as a measure of intimacy with one's spouse, it is possible to fashion a rough and ready empirical test of the nature of the relationship between the two loves. What effect does the prayer life of a young Catholic married couple have on their sex life? I want to note again that such questions, asked in many fashionable and progressive Catholic circles, would lead to ridicule. Prayer is nice, one might be told, and sex is nice, but the two really do not mix.

In approximately a quarter of the Catholic marriages we have studied, both members of the couple pray every day. In 42% of those families, both husband and wife described their sexual fulfillment as "excellent." On the other hand, where one or both of the spouses does not pray every day only 24% described their sexual fulfillment as "excellent." The difference is statistically significant, and the coefficient of association (gamma) is quite high —.50. Prayer and sex do, indeed, mix, and the two loves do, indeed, relate strongly one to another.

Moreover, the association between husbands' and wives' prayer increases with the duration of marriage. The gamma in the early years of marriage is .31. It diminishes to .21 between the third and the eighth year of marriage but then rises to .42 during the last two years of the first decade of marriage. As your story and my story become our story, both of us are more likely to get involved with God (though not necessarily together, since the question merely revealed whether the respondent and the spouse pray every day and not whether they pray together).

Since we know that there is a correlation between warm images and sexual fulfillment, we are not surprised to see that those who have warm images of the cosmic personages are also more likely to communicate with them. Hence, prayer, sexual fulfillment, and warm religious images intercorrelate with one another. The more a husband and wife pray, the more likely they are to have sexually fulfilling marriages, and the warmer the imagery of Those to whom they pray, the more likely they are to have sexually fulfilling marriages. Furthermore, both of these variables, while they are related to each other, also make an independent contribution to each other and are not substitutes for one another.

Greater probability of sexual fulfillment exists in marriages in which there is both daily prayer by the two spouses and warm images in the religious fantasy of the two spouses. Indeed, it is precisely among those marriages in which both spouses pray every day and both spouses have warm images that the difference in sexual fulfillment occurs. More than half of them report excellent sexual fulfillment (by both husband and wife), twice as many as in the other three categories. In the technical parlance of social science, daily prayer *specifies* the difference in sexual fulfillment between those families which share warm imagery and those that do not. It is precisely the combination of the two, in other words, that accounts for the difference in sexual fulfillment in a young Catholic family.

The proportion of Catholic families in which both husband and wife pray every day increases as the marriage goes on. It is not merely, then, that *your* story and *my* story become more closely related, and that *your* story of *your* relationship with God and that *my* story of *my* relationship with God tend to converge. It is also true that *our* joint relationship with God improves through the years of the marriage, just as *our* relationship with one another is improving. As *our* story gets better, so does *our* involvement in God's story become more active.

It is impossible, of course, with our present data to sort out the influence flow between the two loves. St. Paul's difficult syntax as he shifts back and forth manifests the same problem that the researcher faces: the two loves are so closely connected that it is hard to chart the ebb and flow one upon the other. However, if one assumes that there is at least some influence of prayer and warm images on the level of the sexual fulfillment in young Catholic families, one can say that prayer makes an additional contribution to the explanation of the rebound between the middle and late years of marriage and sexual fulfillment. The difference between the third and the eighth year on the one hand and the ninth and the tenth year on the other is twenty-two percentage points. When the warm imagery is taken into account, the difference diminishes to nine percentage points—in other words, three-quarters of the increase in sexual fulfillment can be accounted for by changes in the religious imagery of the spouses between the middle and the end of the first decade of their marriage. When one adds to that the daily prayer of spouses the difference diminishes even more to six percentage points, and one has accounted for three-quarters of the change in sexual fulfillment. Whether religion influences sexuality or sexuality influences religion may be hard to determine. That they both have an extraordinary impact on one another is now beyond any doubt.

Do men and women know that they are being influenced religiously by their mate? One of the questions in the survey asked the respondent to rate a number of potential religious influences on a four point scale (mother, father, friends, priests, etc.). If correlations exist between the conscious rating of the spouse's influence and the family religious styles analyzed in this chapter, then it would follow that not all the husband-wife, wife-husband influence is preconscious or subconscious. In fact, there are statistically significant correlations between the perception of spouse's influence and the joint imagery, joint prayer, and joint sexual fulfillment measures. We cannot say with certainty that there is a consciousness that the spouse is leading the respondent to pray more or to have warmer religious imagery, but there is a consciousness that the spouse is exercising influence.

Furthermore, this influence seems to wane then wax during the first ten years of marriage, as do so many other aspects of the relationship. In the final years of the decade, the spouse's religious influence is more likely to be perceived as strong than during the earlier years. Also, the correlations between imagery and prayer on the one hand and perceived influence of the spouse on the other seem to go through the same "U curve"; the relationship between the perception of the spouse's influence and the joint imagery and joint behavior is strongest during the final years of the first decade of marriage. Not only do joint prayer and joint imagery increase in the "rebound" period, so does the perception of the spouse's influence and the relationship between such a perception and prayer and imagery. Not only are *your* story and *my* story becoming *our* story, but *we* are becoming self-conscious about the fact that it is *our* story.

This might be the description of one possible influence flow: Husband and wife have warm religious images. This sharing of "stories of God" makes it more likely that the two of them will pray frequently. A combination of the "stories" and the mutual (if not common) prayer leads them to perceive that they are having more religious influence on one another. All three factors improve their sexual fulfillment. If one adds self-consciousness about religious influence to the explanatory model developed to explain the "rebound" in sexual fulfillment, then three-quarters of the 22% point increase between the third-eighth and the ninth-tenth year can be accounted for.

Earlier in the chapter it was noted that 52% of those couples both of whom pray every day and both of whom have warm religious images report that their sexual fulfillment is excellent. If one adds self-consciousness about spouse's influence, the percentage rises to 57%—ten percentage points higher than those with images and prayer but without the self-consciousness and thirty-five percentage points higher than the rest of the sample. Thus, not only is there some self-consciousness about religious influence of the spouse, but this self-consciousness heightens the impact of the influence

CONCLUSION

Religious imagery and the sexual relationship interact in subtle and intricate ways in the marriage lives of young Catholics. Not only does the imagery predict sexual fulfillment (a finding that confirms the basic thesis of the present book that what is unique about Catholic marriages is the "analogical" or sacramental image Catholics have of sex despite the repressive words they hear from some of their leaders), but the ebb and flow of marital satisfaction and sexual fulfillment is a function of the ebb and flow of sacramental imagery. In

Chapter Three, I showed that it is precisely this imagery which accounts for the greater "exuberance" of the Catholic experience of sex. This chapter confirms that effect and shows, too, that it is the work of subtle interaction between Catholic spouses in the life cycle of the marriage.

Might this same phenomenon occur among young people who are not Catholic? I cannot say for sure, BUT on the basis of Chapter Three, I can say that "sacramental" religious imagery does not have the same effect on the population of those who are not Catholic, so there is every reason to think it would not have the same impact on the younger generation either.

Sex and the Single Catholic:
The Decline of an Ethic

If their religious story correlates with a story of marital passion for married Catholics, what does the same story do for single Catholics? Can a line be drawn between the two states in life in which the story applies to the married state but not to the single state?

The answer would appear to be, "not any more."

The institutional Church has striven mightily during the last quarter century to protect the Catholic sexual ethic, an ethic which in effect it has interpreted to mean that sexual pleasure can be enjoyed only in marriage and then only with an openness to the possibility of the procreation of children. Authority and sex have been the two crucial issues, often combined into one: the Church's claim to authority over the sexual lives of the faithful.

How has this mighty effort fared in the United States? Three-quarters of Catholic Americans think that extramarital sex is always wrong, a proportion which is the same as that of Americans who are not Catholic and which has not changed since the early 1960s. In a "sealed ballot" survey conducted by NORC, 86% of Americans say that they have been faithful to their spouse, Catholics and others alike. Twenty-six percent of ever-married Catholics have had a divorce as opposed to 32%

of those who are not Catholic. For Catholics in their thirties and forties, the ever-divorced of ever-married rate is 33% while for other Americans it is 44%. (The oft-quoted cliché that half of all marriages will end in divorce is a projection of trends and not a measure of actual divorces.)

Two-thirds of American Catholics believe that homosexuality is always wrong, the same as those who are not Catholic, and with minor fluctuations, this proportion has not changed either. I will make no attempt to analyze gay or lesbian sex in this chapter because of the small number of cases. One percent of women state in the "secret ballot" sealed envelope questionnaire used in the surveys I am working with that they have had sex with members of their own gender during the past year, as do 3% of the men. Moreover, virtually all national sample studies with which I am familiar (including a British study) report the same numbers.

Catholic attitudes on abortion have not changed since 1972: nine out of ten approving of the legality of abortion when the mother's life is in danger and three out of ten approving of abortion on demand. Again, there is no difference between Catholics and Protestants on the abortion issue. Catholic young women are less likely to have an abortion than are other Americans, but nonetheless, one out of six does have an abortion before her middle twenties. The lower Catholic abortion rate is in great part the result of the fact that Catholic women begin sexual activity later than other Americans.

Nine out of ten Catholic Americans do not believe that birth control is wrong. Six out of ten married Catholic women of childbearing age are actually using some form of artificial contraception, though they are more likely to use the pill and less likely to use sterilization than other Americans.

There remains the issue of premarital sex or, as I shall call it in this chapter, "single sex" so as to include the divorced, the separated, and the widowed as well as the never married. If the term "Sexual Revolution" stands for anything at all, it means an increase in single sex, in great part because of the availability of inexpensive and effective birth control devices, especially the pill. There is some doubt about how revolutionary Americans have become. As I will note later in this chapter, single Americans have not become notably promiscuous. Nonetheless, there does appear to have been an increase in single sex. The question then becomes how has this increase and the possible changing cultural values about the role of sex in human life affected Catholic single Americans whose religious story involves a love affair with God?[1]

This chapter, like the first, is based on questions asked about sexual behavior in the General Social Survey (a survey conducted by NORC every year since 1972) for the years 1989-1991. There are 4416 adults over eighteen in the study, of whom 1099 are Catholic. 2044 of these adults are not married of whom 496 are Catholic. The samples are national probability samples and hence provide estimates with a margin of error of a couple of percentage points which will be different from the real population on the average five times out of a hundred.

A DECLINE IN CHASTITY?

It is often said that the sexual behavior of Catholics has been so shaped by American culture that there will be nothing distinctively Catholic about their sexual lives. Respect for chastity, it is implied in such an allegation, will be no higher among Catholics than it is among anyone else. In point of fact, the sexual behavior of single Catholics IS distinctive: Single Catholics are significantly less likely to have been chaste during the last year than single Protestants (34% versus 43%), regardless of the latter's denominational affiliation. (Question: "About how often did you have sex during the past twelve months?" All questions were answered on a "secret ballot" card which was placed in a sealed envelope.) Moreover, 38% of the sexually active single Catholics engage in sexual intercourse every week as opposed to 31% of the sexually active other single Americans.

Thus, only a little more than a third of single Catholics in the United States were chaste during the previous year, and almost two-fifths of those who were not chaste reported sex once a week or more. Not only do married Catholics engage in sex more frequently than do other married Americans, so too, do single Catholics.

Why do single Catholics engage in sex more than do other single Americans? Thirty-three percent of other Americans think that premarital sex is always wrong as opposed to 17% of American Catholics. (Question: "If a man and a woman have sex relations before marriage, do you think it is always wrong, almost always wrong, wrong only sometimes, or not wrong at all?") When this difference in attitude is taken into account, the differences between Catholics and others in both the rate and frequency of single sex disappears. Catholics are more likely to engage in single sex and, once they engage in it, to do so more frequently because they are less likely to think that it is always wrong.

Is this evidence of a "sexual revolution" among single Catholics? One cannot say with certainty because there are no reliable data about frequency of sex among single Catholics in years past. However, there are data from NORC's General Social Survey and its two Parochial School Studies about Catholic attitudes for the last thirty years towards premarital sex. In 1963 at the time of the first NORC Parochial School Study, three out of every four Catholics thought that premarital sex was always wrong as opposed to two-thirds of American Protestants. By 1972, both rates had declined sharply so that only about a third of Americans, regardless of denomination, thought it was always wrong. The Protestant rate has leveled off in the last twenty years at one third believing that premarital sex is always wrong, but the Catholic rate has continued to decline so that at the present time only one out of six American Catholics think that premarital sex is always wrong.

There clearly has been a dramatic change in American attitudes towards premarital sex (perhaps in great part because of the availability of the birth control pill), but the change among Catholics is even more dramatic. The Protestant change stopped twenty years ago, the Catholic change continues even to the present. It would appear that something is happening in Catholic sexual attitudes which is more than merely a change in American culture. A third of the Catholic decline between 1962 and 1974 (in the two Parochial School Studies) can be accounted for by changing attitudes towards Church authority. The collapse of the Catholic sexual ethic above and beyond the social change affecting other Americans seems to be related to a special Catholic rejection of the right of Church authority to dictate on sexual matters—perhaps in response to the 1968 birth control encyclical of Pope Paul VI. Hence, one must raise the question of whether attempts by Church leadership to preserve the Catholic sexual ethic might have been counterproductive.

Moreover, once age is taken into account, single Catholics who are sexually active are as likely to attend church services regularly as are single Catholics who are chaste. Finally, the difference in frequency of sexual activity between single Catholics and other singles can be explained by the impact of a spousal image of God on Catholics—the same impact which accounted for a greater frequency of marital sex among Catholics as described previously.

Once Catholics make up their minds that single sex is not wrong, then their religious story will interact with their sexual story in a fashion which will incline them to more sexual activity than is to be found among single Americans who are not Catholic

It is evident that Catholic leadership has little credibility with its people on the subject of single sex. A large proportion of Catholics no longer accept the thesis that sexual pleasure must be limited to married persons who are open in each sexual act to the possibility of procreation.

FREE LOVE UNBOUND?

Does the decline of the Catholic sexual ethic mean that Catholics have become promiscuous? Has an era of free love dawned for American Catholics? Has the *Playboy* philosophy become the new ethic of the Catholic population? Has complete sexual permissiveness taken over in America?

The data in the General Social Survey suggest that the answers to all of these questions is a resounding "no." Seventy percent of single Americans (the data on Catholics in this section does not indicate a significant difference between them and other Americans) who are sexually active report that they had only one sexual partner during the past year—91% of the widowed, 66% of the divorced, and 57% of the never-married.

Moreover, four out of five describe this one partner as a "regular" sexual partner. (Question: "Was one of the partners your husband or wife or regular sexual partner?") Thus half of sexually active single Americans say that they have had sex with only one partner during the past year and that person is their "regular" sexual partner—80% of the widowed, 60% of the divorced or separated, and 46% of the never married. If one defines a "liaison" as a relationship with one person who is considered a "regular" sexual partner not unlike a spouse (because of its linkage with a spouse in the question wording), then 45% of the sexually active in their twenties are in liaisons, 55% of those in their thirties, 58% of those in their forties, 71% of those in their fifties, and 69% of those over sixty.

Of single American Catholics, approximately one third are chaste, one third are in liaison relationships, and another third are sexually active but not in liaisons—though a quarter of the latter have had only one sexual partner in the last year.

"Sexual permissiveness" seems to mean for most single Americans who are sexually active one sexual partner to whom one is bound by some sort of quasi-commitment of de facto if not necessarily permanent fidelity. Indeed, two-thirds of those single persons who claim a regular sexual partner (85% of the sexually active singles) have been faithful to their partner during the past year. "Free love," one must remark, this is not.

We do not know from the GSS data whether those with only one sexual partner are living together or whether they are contemplating marriage. Perhaps fidelity among unmarried lovers results from the logistic and emotional problems that promiscuity involves. Perhaps, too, a bond, almost as powerful as the marriage bond, develops between such faithful single lovers. It is known from other research that the breaking of this bond can be as traumatic as divorce among married people. It is also known that living together before marriage correlates negatively with marital success, perhaps because those who live together before marriage tend to come from backgrounds which are not conducive to marital success. Nonetheless, it would appear that an emergent ethic among many single Americans regards sex as designed for monogamous bonding in quasi-permanent and quasi-committed relationships which differ from married relationships only in that a public commitment to fidelity and permanency has not (yet) been made.

It may also not be all that new. To what extent, I wonder, is the common law marriage recognized by the pre-Tridentine Church to be seen as a useful model for considering liaison relationships? At many times and in many places in Catholic history, particularly in the rural areas among the servi and the coloni (serfs and colonists, the latter even lower on the social class scale than the former), this must have been the typical Catholic marriage. It would seem that the only religious difference between the common law marriage of the past and the liaisons of the present (in which there is an intent of one sort or another to marry eventually) is the Tridentine legislation requiring an exchange of vows in the presence of the parish priest and two witnesses, a requirement for the "form" of marriage imposed rather late in this country.

As a sociologist, I note merely that the model of pre-Tridentine common law liaisons suggests that the single sex relationships which have resulted from the so-called "sexual revolution" do not seem all that revolutionary or all that new.

CONCLUSION

The ethic which seems to be the basis for single sex among American Catholics at the present differs from the traditional Catholic ethic not in that the former does not value either fidelity or monogamy or even a propensity towards permanence. It differs rather, first of all, in its willingness to make a definitive public commitment to these characteristics. It also differs in that it does not believe that every sexual act should be "open" to the possibility of procreation (in that no obstacle is placed in the way of procreation). In the latter respect, however, the ethic for single sex among American Catholics does not differ from the ethic for marital sex. Catholic laity—single and married—seem to have chosen an ethical perspective which emphasizes the bonding function of sex, while the leadership of the Church still emphasizes the procreative function, however much it may have changed the rhetoric of this emphasis. When the stories are different, the story contained in the Popular Tradition will usually win.

On the other hand, both single and married Catholics seem to have fewer sexual hang-ups than do other Americans, apparently because the spousal image of God has a special impact on sexual behavior among Catholics. The religious story both shapes the sexual story and is shaped by it, regardless of whether one is a married Catholic or a single Catholic. The ethic has changed, the story seems to remain the same.

The Confidant Relationship

The Catholic priesthood is under assault in the 1990s, partly because, as I shall note in the next chapter, of its failure to deal honestly and penitently with the problem of sexual abuse of children by priests. In particular, the celibacy of priests is being subjected to heavy weapon fire of criticism. Most priests are not mature celibates, according to ex-priest R. W. Richard Sipe. Celibacy is the cause of sexual abuse of children by priests, many newspaper and television analyses of the problem say or imply. Celibacy is not a natural life, yet others insist (again especially those who have forsworn their priestly commitments). Celibates cannot understand women, angry Catholic feminists proclaim. Morale is terrible, many priests will tell you, and it won't get better until the Church changes on celibacy.

Much of this is babble, some of it is hysteria, and some of it is anti-Catholic screed. Sipe's study—based on, he tells us, five-hundred clinical interviews, five-hundred workshops, and five-hundred conversations with priests—is, from the point of view of valid statistical estimation, garbage (and would not be taken seriously if it were on some other subject). The study by Thomas Nestor at Loyola University of the occupational and career and personal satisfactions of a random sample (which Sipe lacks) of Chicago priests has demonstrated that the morale of priests is higher than that of a comparable sample of married laymen (which Sipe didn't have either).

It is not my purpose in this book, however, to engage in controversy about celibacy. It might well be wise to make exceptions to the rule at the present time—though it will sure not happen during the present regime in Rome. Rather, I propose to consider from the Young Catholic study, a special aspect of celibacy, the confidant relationship between a married woman and a priest and the impact of that relationship on the woman and her marriage.

Undoubtedly, some priests have exploited women who come to them seeking advice about their marriages. (Perhaps the opposite has also happened.) But there is more that must be said. In the absence of celibacy the benign chemistry of the confidant relationship might well be lost.

While young Catholic women with "feminist" propensity are alienated from Church leadership, they do not seem to be alienated from their own local clergy. It would appear from the argument presented in this chapter that the antagonism is towards the "hierarchy," perhaps even towards the "Vatican," but not toward the lower clergy. On the contrary, it seems that Catholic married women have helpful relationships with their local clergy, the sort that cannot be found in other religious denominations.

There are virtually no differences between women and men (whether married or unmarried) in their judgments as to whether their parish priest is very sympathetic, and in their having had a conversation with a priest about a religious problem during the past year, and saying that a priest has had a considerable impact on their thinking about the Catholic faith.

The last two items were combined into a factor which taps both recent conversations with a priest and agreement that a priest has had a powerful religious effect on one's life. The scale correlates positively with marital satisfaction, both for the wife and for the family unit. If a woman is high on the scale, both she and her husband are more likely to say that their marriage is very satisfactory. Far from being a rival to the husband, then, it would appear that the celibate priest is a positive asset to his marriage relationship.

This effect seems only to exist for women. The more likely a woman is to have an influential and recent relationship with a priest, the more likely she is to be very satisfied with her marriage (74% versus 64%) while a man's relationship with a priest does not increase the quality of his marital satisfaction. However, the woman's relationship does increase the joint satisfaction of husband and wife with their marriage. If the woman has neither had a recent conversation with a priest nor has been strongly influenced religiously in her life by a priest, only half the couples will both say they are very satisfied with their marriage. If her relationship with a priest is both recent and influential, however, 72% of the couples will say they are very satisfied with their marriage. Note that both recent time of the contact with a priest and strong influence by a priest are required for the effect on joint marital satisfaction. One without the other makes little difference in marital satisfaction for husband and wife.

The "confidant" relationship also correlates with positive psychological well-being significantly for women and not significantly for men, but only for married women, a little more than one-third of whom are high on the positive psychological well-being scale if they have no contact with a priest, and almost two-thirds of whom are high on the scale if they do have a confidant relationship.

Thus, although only one out of every seven married Catholic women has a priest "confidant"—she has had a recent conversation with the priest about religious matters and reports that a priest has had an important religious influence on her life—such women are likely to be higher on the score of positive well-being and to be involved in marriages in which both the wife and husband are satisfied with the quality of the relationship.

The question naturally arises as to whether this apparently satisfactory relationship happens despite the celibacy of the priest or because of it. Can such relationships be found in other denominations?

Since the data in the General Social Survey provide no methods for directly addressing this question, one must use an indirect and tentative argument which is presented as speculative exploration and not a certain proof. The technique is based on a GSS measure of confidence in religious leadership. In Young Catholic study, young Catholic women who have high confidence in their organizational leadership are more likely to say that they are very satisfied with their marriage than those who have low confidence in their religious leadership. However, this seems to be entirely the result of the fact that some such women have a confidant relationship with a priest. Those who lack a confidant relationship and have a great deal of confidence in Church leadership are lower in marital satisfaction than those who have low confidence in Church leadership. Without the intervention of a priest, confidence in Church leadership correlates negatively with marital satisfaction for Catholic women. If you are very confident in Church leadership, your marriage is less satisfactory unless there is a priest "confidant" involved who seems to be able to reverse the direction of the relationship.

Returning to the GSS, we find that the significant positive correlation between confidence in Church leadership and marital satisfaction for women exist only among Roman Catholics. It is not statistically significant for the other denominations. Now since we have already determined from the Young Catholic study that the reason why there is a positive relationship between marital satisfaction and confidence in Church leadership for Catholic married women is the intervention of a priest confidant, we may speculate that the absence of a significant relationship in the other denominations may well be the result of an absence of an intervening clerical confidant.

Minimally it can be said with confidence that the celibacy of the priest is not an obstacle to explaining the confidant relationship, and there are strong hints that it may be a positive asset.

One might further speculate that for Catholic young married women a friendly and trusting relationship with another man in which there is little "danger" and considerable encouragement, social support, and reassurance leaves her more free and less tense for the relationship with her husband. It may well be that the ability to provide such relationships for married women is one of the unperceived but important functions of clerical celibacy (it might be added that those of us who have worked as parish priests have intuitively been aware of this function for a long time). It also may be that the absence of a counterpart relationship for young Catholic married men could be a pragmatic argument for the ordination of women—though if our speculative reasons about the importance of celibacy for such relationships is correct, then it would follow that this function would only be achieved with a celibate women clergy.

What is there about a confidant relationship between a priest and a young married woman which facilitates the marital happiness of both she and her husband? A confidant relationship does not improve the woman's estimate of the sexual fulfillment in her marriage (.04). However, it does improve her husband's propensity to say that the sexual fulfillment is excellent (.11). A confidant relationship correlates not with the wife's sexual fulfillment but with the husband's. If the woman has what may well be a supportive friendship with a priest, it improves the quality of her husband's sexual satisfaction. Furthermore, when these three variables are put into a regression equation, it develops that the sexual fulfillment of the husband is indeed the intervening variable linking the confidant relationship with a priest and the marital satisfaction of the wife. A wife's marital satisfaction is improved by a confidant relationship with a priest precisely because that relationship tends to enhance the sexual fulfillment of her husband.

A possible explanation for this phenomenon is that if a young wife receives sufficient encouragement from the priest to be open to her own sexuality, she abandons some of her inhibitions and is able, therefore, to be a more satisfying sexual partner to her husband. If such be the dynamics of the relationship, they certainly ought to be examined much more closely in future research. It would appear that I have found an interesting manifestation of a "latent function" of clerical celibacy and also perhaps another pragmatic argument for the importance of a counterpart "confidant" for married men—a celibate woman priest!

What kind of priest do such women seek out for confidant relationships? Those in such relationships are much more likely to rate priests' sermons as excellent, to describe priests as very understanding, to be in parishes where there is a good deal of activity and where priests do not expect laity to be followers. They are also substantially more likely to endorse the piety, concern, and the training of their professional clergy. It would appear, therefore, that the confidant relationships exist in parishes which are active and have democratic leaderships, where the counseling skills are excellent and where the priests are pious, committed, and well-trained. Presumably, these are precisely the kind of qualities a young woman would look for in the priest "confidant."

When the ratings of priest performance are subjected to a factor analysis, two scales emerge—one that measured the social and political activism of a priest, and the other his piety, concern, professional preparation, and democratic style. The social activism factor correlated neither positively nor negatively with the confidant relationship. However, the "professionalism" of the priest did correlate positively and significantly: the women who are high on the scale estimating the "professionalism" of their parish clergy were twice as likely to have confidant relationships.

(There was no relationship between "feminism" and "confidant" relationship. Those who are high on the "feminism" scale and those who were low were equally as likely to have such a relationship. Young women's perception that Church leadership wishes to keep them in an inferior status does not seem to have any effect on their propensity to enter confidant relationships with the priests.)

The materials presented in this chapter are extremely tentative. We do not know, for example, that the priest with whom the married woman has talked recently is the same priest who has had a notable impact on her life. Nor can we be sure that celibacy is an asset in developing the clergyman/woman relationship. Finally, it is possible that it is precisely those women who are in satisfactory marriages and whose husbands are satisfied with the quality of their sexual relationship who would feel free to choose a religious relationship with a priest, so the causal connection may flow in the opposite direction than the one assumed in this chapter. This seems less likely than the relationship postulated in the chapter but certainly cannot be excluded until further research is done. Nevertheless, despite their antagonism towards higher Church leaders, it is clear that young Catholic married women are able to have satisfying relationships with their priests, relationships which are at least linked to, if indeed do not promote, happier marriages.

What effect does a confidant relationship have on a young Catholic married woman's attitudes towards change in the clerical life? Such women are more "liberal" than those who lack such relationships on the matter of ordination of women. Fifty-five percent of them think such a change is important as opposed to forty percent of those without a confidant. On the other hand, they are less likely to support permission for a married clergy—48 percent of the "confidant" women support such a change as opposed to 60 percent of those who lack a confidant.

Clearly, the confidant women are not reactionaries on the subject of women priests, yet they favor the retention of clerical celibacy, perhaps because they perceive—however dimly—that their own beneficial relationship with a priest is in part the result of his celibate status. Perhaps one of the reasons why they strongly support the other change is that they perceive that their husbands might benefit from a similar relationship with a celibate woman priest.

Furthermore—and perhaps astonishingly—exactly the same pattern exists among the husbands. Those with wives in confidant relationships are more likely to support the ordination of women and less likely than those whose wives lack such relationships to advocate optional celibacy—as though they, too, perceive the enhancement to their lives of a celibate priest counselor for their wives—and perhaps even the additional enhancement which would occur if they had a celibate woman priest as their own "confidant."

Obviously these speculations are very tentative, but they point in the direction of inquiries which are extremely important for the future of the priesthood and the future of the Church.

The final question to be asked is whether it is precisely those husbands and wives who have benefited from the confidant relationship who are the most likely to be in favor of celibacy and also in favor of the ordination of women. Are those whose marriages have been positively affected by a wife's relationship with a priest most reluctant to see celibacy abandoned but also most eager to have women priests (from whom, possibly, men can derive similar benefits as their wives have from relationships with celibate priests)?

Admittedly, this is a very long-shot question. It supposes that the relationship demonstrated in the previous paragraphs is to be found ONLY among those whose marriages have profited from confidant relationships and that for others in which there is a confidant relationship the situation will reverse itself. It assumes that if a table is created in which those who are in confidant relationships (or whose wives are) and those who are high on marital satisfaction (or in the husband's case on sexual fulfillment) represent the upper left-hand cell, the proportion in that cell will be higher than in the other cells on the subject of the ordination of women (above half) and lower than those in other cells in support of optional celibacy (less than half).

Yet this is precisely what occurs. The highest support for women priests and the strongest opposition to optional celibacy comes from those husbands and wives who have benefited (either in marital satisfaction in the wife's case or sexual fulfillment in the husband's) from a wife's confidant relationship with a priest. (See chapter table.)

The implications of this phenomenon for the social psychology and sociology of the celibate state are enormous. There is something in the "chemistry" of the relationship between a priest and a married woman which establishes an "electricity" often beneficial to both the wife and her husband and makes both of them more committed to celibacy and more committed to the ordination of women. The phenomenon ought to be studied in much greater detail but will doubtless be ignored. The left wing will not tolerate anything good to be said about celibacy, and the right wing will not tolerate the thought that there is a special "chemistry" between the celibate and the married woman (and possibly between a celibate woman and a married man).

Ridicule does not refute a finding, it merely dismisses it. I see no one in the Church today, on any of the sides of the celibacy controversy, who is prepared to take my research on the confidant relationship seriously—despite the power of the findings. The Vatican insists on the rules. The critics of celibacy insist on the end of the rule. No one wants to hear about some of the positive effects of celibacy.

No one wants to be told that celibacy is a component of the Catholic experience of sex, and a positive component at that.

TABLE

Wife's Attitudes Toward Changes in the Clergy by Confidant Status and Marital Satisfaction

	Marital Happiness	
	High	Low
Percent Pro Optional Celibacy:		
Has a Confidant	47%	64%
Has not	62%	57%
Percent Pro Women Priests:		
Has a Confidant	61%	41%
Has not	41%	42%

Sexual Abuse:
The Dimensions of the Problem

The sexual abuse of children by priests must be factored into any discussion of the Catholic experience of sex. Although such abuse has become a public scandal in the early 1990s, it has been going on a long time. How can the Church have been so stern about the natural sexual pleasures of the laity and so tolerant of the sexual perversions of the clergy? Does not the corruption revealed in the reassignment of such priests to parishes where they will find other victims indicate a perversity in the institutional Church, which offends not only victims, not only the whole Catholic tradition of the sacramentality of sex which this book has been exploring, but plain common ordinary decency and honesty?

My answer to both those questions is yes. Other institutions in which professionals have easy access to young people have a similar problem. Other institutions also do their best to cover up the problem. But very few knowingly reassign child abusers to future work with children. The institutional Church, up to and including the Vatican, has become so twisted in this thinking about human sexuality and has so forgotten the sacramental popular tradition that it seems to have been capable of any enormity so long as it could be justified on the grounds that it was for the good of the Church and the good of the priesthood.

After the publication of Jason Berry's monumental study of sexual abuse by priests, *Lead US Not Into Temptation: Catholic Priests and the Sexual Abuse of Children,* (Doubleday, 1992), certain voices were raised in the Catholic community which suggested that the problem might not be as bad as the public image suggests and that it was under control. None of these voices denied that a problem existed. They cited the distinction between pedophiles and ephebophiles made by some therapists who treat priests; they blamed the media for exaggerating the problem; all express some skepticism about the charges being made (a climate of growing skepticism about whether the acts were committed at all). All worried about the assault on celibacy involved in the sexual abuse charges; one voice seemed to take consolation from the fact that some of the allegations concern events that happened fifteen or thirty years ago. None, if I may say so, exhibited any sense of the life-long horror such assaults produce in their victims. All seemed designed to reassure laity and to protect the Church and the clergy from unjust attack, the same motives which led bishops to cover up sexual abuse cases in the past.

In the face of this commentary from very different sources, it seemed appropriate to raise the question of just how serious the sexual abuse crisis is. To answer that question, I proposed a number of subordinate questions about the facts of the matter as we now know them or may not unreasonably project them.

1. How many priests are guilty of sexual abuse of children and minors?

In the Archdiocese of Chicago where a three-person commission reviewed the clergy files for allegations made in the last quarter century, thirty-nine priests were judged to have been the subjects for valid accusations. Some of the men were dead or had left the priesthood; the remaining twenty-one were removed from the active ministry and will not be reassigned to regular parish work (as were two more subsequently). They remain in limbo awaiting a determination as to whether they will ever be permitted to act as priests again.

The twenty-five cases represent approximately 3.27% of the 763 men who were active priests in Chicago[1] at the time of the removal The commission did not reveal its criteria for decisions. Allegations persist against other priests for whom the Church or the civil society does not so far think that there is enough evidence to justify action. A priest who has subsequently been indicted was not reviewed by the commission because, apparently, there was not enough evidence in his file to justify such a review. Some sexual abuse activists claim that there are as many as seventy priests against whom allegations have been made.

I do not propose in this chapter to question either the good faith of those who claim the Cardinal's commission's work was inadequate or of the commission. I will be content with the conservative conclusion that the proportion of one out of ten priests as sexual abusers might be too high and one out of twenty might be too low.

When this .0327 is multiplied by 52,277 active priests in the United States (on the assumption that the Chicago diocesan rate does not differ greatly from that of other priests, diocesan and religious order), the result is seventeen hundred and nine priests who would have been removed last year if the Chicago review method were applied nationally. If one accepts the Vatican's admission that charges have been made against four hundred priests by the summer of 1993, it follows that there were some thirteen hundred abusers still active in the priestly ministry at that time.

2. How many children and minors have been victims of sexual abuse?

The projections in the previous section are simple arithmetic. A more difficult question for which to estimate an answer is how many victims does each such abuser have? Dr. Gene Abel in his research on 571 pedophiles reported that each had on the average 380 victims. It is claimed that most priests guilty of sexual abuse are not pedophiles in the strict sense but ephebophiles: their victims are not children but adolescents. I have some doubts about this distinction. However, even if only one out of ten priest abusers is a pedophile in the strict sense—170 priests—their victims, assuming Abel's rate, would number more than sixty thousand children.

If one estimates that on the average each priest abuser has fifty victims, then one can project more than eighty-five thousand victims. Or to use another model, assuming that one out of ten priest abusers is a true pedophile and the other nine are ephebophiles with, let us say, only ten victims, one can project approximately eighty thousand victims of men who were in the priesthood last year.

When one adds the victims of men who have left the priesthood through either death or resignation over the last quarter century, the figure of a hundred thousand does not seem an unreasonable estimate—each one a human being who has suffered a terrible personal tragedy at the hands of a slayer of the soul.

3. What kind of priests sexually abuse children and minors?

The answer is badly troubled men with powerful and sometimes irresistible compulsions. As one authority puts it, they have vandalized love maps, that is, their sexual development was itself violated so that their love target is inappropriate. Often they were victimized themselves in childhood. Medical science understands very little about the various forms of paraphilia. The typology of pedophile/ephebophile is little more than a distinction based on the age of the love target. Some men focus on children regardless of gender and are not homosexual in the ordinary sense of that word; others are homosexuals whose target of preference is an adolescent boy; still others are heterosexuals whose target of preference is an adolescent girl. (Neither of the latter two justify either gay bashing or straight bashing.) Still others enjoy humiliating the victim rather than the sexual pleasure itself. The medical literature is not hopeful about recovery for any of these victimizers, especially those whose focus is children. The claim made by some Catholic institutions to have rehabilitated ephebophiles through techniques like those used by Alcoholics Anonymous should be treated with serious reservation, especially when there is a possibility of assigning such men to priestly work again. Repentance and reconciliation ought to be balanced against the serious risk to potential victims.

4. How much money have these victimizers cost the Church?

The Archdiocese of Chicago, taking the lead in candor, admitted in 1993 that it had paid out 1.8 million dollars in the previous year for settlements, legal costs, and treatment for survivors and victimizers and that the cost will go up this year and in years to come. On the basis of this number, fifty million dollars a year and rising does not seem to be an unreasonable estimate of costs to the Church—to the lay person that is, who contributes to the Sunday collection.

5. Are Catholic priests the only sexual abusers of children and minors?

Most sexual abuse victims are girls and young women abused by their fathers and other male relatives. While girls and young women have been abused by priests, most of the victims of priests are boys and young men. Police experts insist that most abusers of boys and young men are, in fact, married men. Protestant and Jewish denominations are faced with the same problem. I am told that Lutheran bishops estimate they spend a quarter of their time on sexual abuse cases, as compared to thirty percent of his time as estimated by Cardinal Joseph Bernardin. Sexual abuse is a possibility in any area in which men have an opportunity to work with children or minors—education, scouting, athletics. Are there more priests who are guilty of such behavior than clergy in other denominations or men working in other professions? Perhaps, perhaps not. In any case, Catholic priests have no monopoly on sexual abuse of children. Why then are they targets of special media attention? Because, as Cardinal Bernardin has remarked, their celibate commitment holds them in the mind of the public to higher standards.

6. Does clerical celibacy cause the sexual abuse
   problem?

Despite all the suggestions by the anti-celibacy crusaders (like
A.W. Richard Sipe), it ought to be evident from the previous
answer that it does not. Those whose love maps compel them
to target children and minors acquire the compulsion early
in their own life experience, long before the seminary and
ordination. Most such men outside of the priesthood are
married. Abolishing celibacy would not solve the problem. I
disagree with Jason Berry on this point: I do not believe that
the clerical culture cover-up syndrome is the result of celibacy
because it has existed in other denominations, too. The
celibacy issue is a red herring manufactured by the media and
such experts as Sipe.

7. Has the incidence of sexual abuse of children
   by Catholic priests increased?

The incidents collated in the review of the Chicago files, I am
told, are rather evenly distributed across the quarter century—
though the reports of such incidents are concentrated in more
recent years. The change seems to be in the willingness of
parents and survivors to come forward with allegations of
sexual misconduct and in the willingness of the media to
become the court of last resort for survivors and families who
have been stonewalled by the Church. There is a vast backlog
of such cases. Even where every attempt has been made to
remove guilty priests, more cases will certainly surface in the
months and years ahead. The cover-ups of the past sewed the
wind. Now the Church reaps the whirlwind.

8. the problem grown worse because of the
   increase of homosexuals in the priesthood?

It's hard to say. My best guess is that there might be some
slight increase in victimization because of the (alleged)
increased number of homosexual priests, if only because a
tiny fraction of gay men view young men (legal minors) as
their preferred or even essential love target. However, it
remains to be proven that the link, should there be one, is

important. The emphasis on it in public discussion only obscures the problem of sexual abuse (and is unfair to celibate gay priests). Incidentally, such estimates as Sipe's that a quarter of priests are gay are little more than guesswork (and his is based on data which any responsible social scientist must dismiss as worthless because of invalid sample design— among other reasons).

9. Are seminaries part of the problem?

Psychologist Eugene Kennedy has suggested that it might be necessary to close down the seminaries to solve the sexual abuse problem. It might be wiser, if less dramatic, to do far more elaborate pre-admission and pre-ordination screening than is currently practiced—something more than a conversation with a psychologist and the administration of the Minnesota Multiphasic Personality Inventory (MMPI) test.

10. What does Rome think about the problem?

As far as I can determine, not much. It has refused the American bishops permission to dismiss victimizers from the priesthood—apparently figuring that the problem is just one more manifestation of American degeneracy. In fact, cases are turning up in other countries, including Ireland; the Vatican is kidding itself if it thinks the problem is not part of the human condition.

11. How does the sexual abuse scandal effect the laity?

The mother of a survivor on T.V. news reporter Bill Kurtis's "Investigative Report" said, tears in her eyes, "I won't let them take my faith away from me." That seems to be the attitude of many of the survivors and their families. They can make the distinction between their heritage on the one hand and the abuse by priests and the brutality by the institutional Church on the other. *The Boston Globe* survey of Catholic laity in the wake of the Father James R. Porter scandal reveals anger, a desire to have the mess cleaned up, more caution about children and priests, and no loss of faith. The laity seem to be coping better than either the clergy or those journalists who worry about lay reaction. Having put up with so much from the Church and its leaders for the last third of a century, the laity apparently can stomach almost anything. However, the Boston survey also revealed an inclination of some Catholics to protest the only way they can—in their collection envelopes.

12. How does the sexual abuse scandal affect the clergy?

The hierarchy is ahead of the clergy. A substantial proportion know they have a grimly serious problem on their hands and are in the process of doing something about it, however belatedly and however reluctantly. Most priests on the other hand are still engaged in denial. Thus, the Association of Chicago Priests will not issue an expression of regret to the survivors and their families and seem concerned only about the privacy of priests, the Cardinal's hot line for sexual abuse complaints, and the rights of priests over/against bishops. There is no reason to think that priests in other dioceses are any different.

13. What needs to be done?

The commentators who are concerned about exaggeration worry about false charges as do priests. Indeed, both groups are more worried about false accusations than about victims or potential victims. In fact, the Church cannot clear the innocent unless it has a process which will also provide practical certainty about the guilty. Hence, independent review boards with more laity on them then clergy (a notion which was first advanced, as far as I know, by one of the Chicago parents who is being sued for libel by Church-supported lawyers) are essential They must be authentically independent—and not just reflections of what they think a bishop wants. Such boards (the Chicago board has six lay persons—five of them women—and three priests) can in time achieve credibility in the larger community. They begin their work unfortunately after the victimization has occurred. Moreover, priests must assume responsibility for policing themselves and reporting sexual abuse by fellow priests to both Church and civil authorities. Finally, priests must take a firm stand in favor of the right of the laity to be free from the fear that their children will be abused by priests.

14. Will the scandal blow over?

It is unlikely to go away for a long time. There is too great a backlog of abuse in the population. Moreover, physical abuse that was not formally sexual in Catholic institutions in years past is another chicken which seems about to come home to roost. I have on my desk an affidavit from a man who claims to have been savagely beaten by a priest, now an important figure in a major diocese, in a Catholic institution many years ago. That corporal punishment was part of Catholic life as recently as the early 1960s is well known to anyone who grew up in that era. (My high school—a preparatory seminary—was unique among the schools my male classmates attended because the faculty was explicitly forbidden to lay violent hands on the students.) But because everyone did it, it does not follow that it was right. Nor does it follow that there was not a sexual component in some of it.

My answers to these questions are, I think, as close to the data and the facts of the sexual abuse problem as one can get at the present time. I admit that I'm on the side of the survivors—at least a few priests should be, given our propensity to maintain that we are on the side of the oppressed. I'm also on the side of the priesthood which I believe can go beyond this problem when priests become mature enough to acknowledge that it exists, apologize for what has happened, and promise that they will do all in their power to see that it doesn't happen again.

In summary, how serious does the sexual abuse problem seem in light of these answers? Every reader must answer that for herself/himself. How serious is the fact of a hundred thousand rapes of children and minors by priests over a quarter century?

Go figure.

Marital Infidelity in the United States

Helen Fisher[1] in her book *The Anatomy of Love* argues that the human propensities to love, attachment, monogamy, and adultery are in part conditioned (though not determined) by evolutionary selection mechanisms which originated among early hominids and pre-hominids.[2] The argument is neither reductionist nor unpersuasive, but questions remain as to how many married men and women in a modern industrial society like the United States actually indulge in the pre-hominid propensity to adultery, who these men and women are, and why the propensity may be especially appealing to them. Results of non-random survey research would indicate that the majority of men and women in the United States have been unfaithful. However, data collection by the National Opinion Research Center in a national probability sample indicates that 10% of American women and 20% of American men have been unfaithful to their spouses.

INFIDELITY RATES

Alfred Kinsey in his famous reports asserted that about half the men and a quarter of the women in his samples had committed adultery. Writing in *Playboy*, Morton Hunt reported that 42% of the white middle-class men and 25% of white middle class women had engaged in adultery. Linda Wolfe in *Cosmopolitan* claimed that 54% of married women had at least one affair. Shere Hite in her report argued that 72% of married men had been adulterous. The June 1987 issue of *Marriage and Divorce* stated confidently that "seventy percent of all Americans engage in an affair sometime during their marital life." Most recently, Samuel S. Janus and Cynthia L. Janus in their *Janus Report on Sexual Behavior in America* report that a third of the married men and a quarter of the married women have been unfaithful to their spouses.

All of these statistics have one characteristic in common: they are not based on national probability samples. In addition, several of them seem to be based on self-selected samples. That a responsible and cautious scholar like Helen Fisher has to rely on articles in *Playboy* and *Cosmopolitan* for data is proof that American social science, largely because of the timidity of funding agencies, has not been able to approach human sexual behavior with all the resources of modern research techniques.

All of these reports are to responsible social science what alchemy is to chemistry, phrenology is to physiology, astrology is to astronomy, and magic is to medicine. Let it be written in the sky: valid statistical inference is possible only from random probability samples. It is essential for randomness that whenever someone is chosen from the population for the sample all other members of the population have a mathematically equal chance of being chosen.

On the basis of a national sample telephone interview (based on random digit dialing) conducted by the Gallup organization, I argued in my book *Faithful Attraction* that nine out of ten Americans claimed to have been faithful to their spouses. However, it seemed possible that respondents would not tell the truth about adultery in a phone interview.

INCIDENCE

As part of its 1991 General Social Survey, NORC asked a battery of questions on sexual behavior of a national probability sample of Americans, 1212 of whom were either married or previously married (widowed, divorced, separated). These questions were answered on a "secret ballot" which was returned to the interviewer in a sealed envelope. In response to the question, "Have you ever had sex with someone other than your husband or wife while you were married?"[3] 11% of the women respondents and 21% of the men replied that they had indeed engaged in sex with someone other than their spouse.

For those who had ever been divorced, the rates rose to 16% for women and 33% for men. For those who had separated from their spouse, the rates in the last twelve months were 35% for women and 57% for men.

Thirty percent of those who admit to having sex with someone other than their spouse also report more than one sexual partner in the previous twelve months, suggesting that for them the infidelity is current. However, 95% of the married men and 98% of the married women have had no more than one sexual partner during the last twelve months.

The national average of 15% unfaithful is much closer to my 10% than it is to the rates cited by many of the authors mentioned above.

Little purpose is served by defending the superiority of probability samples and careful interviews over less stringent techniques in response to those who dismiss these numbers as too low. Moreover, if it is argued that the GSS respondents are lying, one can only reply that if they are then all attempts to study human sexual behavior through interviews (*any* interview and not just survey interviews) are doomed to failure.

It is worth observing, however, that the adultery rate rises to no more than 25% for those who have no religious affiliation, and among the one-fifth of married respondents who do not think that it is always wrong, the rate rises to 35%. Sixty-five percent of those who say that sometimes adultery may not be immoral—and hence would not feel shame or guilt over the act—still assert that they have not engaged in it. At a minimum therefore, one must conclude that the norm in favor of marital fidelity is very powerful in the United States.

Finally, even if one grants that the GSS data reflect only a response pattern and not reality, it remains a more accurate estimate of the response pattern than do the estimates based on previous non-representative surveys.

Are the GSS estimates unreasonable? Do Americans deceive survey interviewers about their sexual behavior? On the basis of comparisons with studies in three other countries—Denmark, France, and Great Britain—one must answer that if deceptions are taking place they are happening systematically in different countries. If they are lying to interviewers, Americans are not the only ones that lie; the Danes and the French and the British do, too. While recent studies of sexual behavior in those three countries, focused as they were on the AIDS problem and condom use as a solution, do not report cross tabulations by marital status (apparently not perceiving that marital fidelity protects far more people from AIDS than condoms do), the proportions reporting no more than one sexual partner in the last year (and for Britain the last five years) are in the same range for all countries. In fact, the British and the French seem marginally more inclined to monogamy. Monogamy rates for the United States are 86%, for Denmark 80%, for Britain 89% and for France 92%. For the last five years the monogamy rates in the United States are 71% and for Britain 68%.

PREVALENCE

Adultery does not correlate with education, religious affiliation or region. For African Americans the infidelity rate is 18% for women and 39% for men. For Hispanics the rates are 8% for women and 46% for men (but there are only 60 Hispanics in the sample, and hence, these figures should be viewed skeptically). Gender then is the most consistent predictor of differential infidelity rates. How can this phenomenon be explained, especially since, as Fisher demonstrates in her review of ethnographic studies, women seem to be as prone to adultery as men in most non-farming cultures?

Perhaps men have more opportunity to find sexual partners, either in the work place or with prostitutes. Indeed, when occupational status and "paid sex" ("Thinking about the time since your 18th birthday, have you ever had sex with a person you paid or paid you for sex?") are taken into account, the difference in adultery rates between the genders goes away (18% of the men and 1% of the women report paid sex). Fifteen percent of both working women and men who have never paid for sex report that they have had sex with someone other than their spouse. As the proportion of women in the work force increases, adultery rates for women will probably increase.

Has adultery increased in America, perhaps as part of a "sexual revolution" (which, with 85% faithful to their spouse, cannot be all that revolutionary)? The question cannot be answered confidently until time series data are available, though as noted in the previous paragraph, the increase in adultery among working women suggests that there has been a change for women.

In the absence of longitudinal data, a possible interpretation of Figure 1 is that the increase in infidelity rates for women from 5% for those over 50 to 15% of those under 50 is the result of more sexual opportunity (and/or perhaps more sexual harassment) for working women whose numbers have increased among the younger cohorts. It may also be that the increase from 25% to 30% for men in their forties (as compared to men in their fifties) represents an increase in infidelity for men. The different patterns for men and women might be accounted for by the fact that adultery increases gradually for men with age and duration of marriage whereas it is a pattern of behavior which emerges early in a marriage for women and remains consistent throughout the marriage— taking into account the increase attributable to more work force participation for women.

The peaks in both lines (in their twenties for women and their forties for men) may well predict the average in years to come—an increase but a modest increase in marriage-long infidelity rates for both men and women.

The difference between working and non-working women appear to be concentrated among those who are in their forties and fifties, perhaps because after forty opportunities go down for women who do not work and increase, as might the motivation, for women who do work. Thus, one might speculate that as more women enter the work force the life-long infidelity rates for women might tend towards 20%.

If these speculative interpretations suggested for the age/gender patterns are valid and if the pattern of those currently in their forties becomes normative for American society, in years to come the adultery rate in the course of life for men would increase to 30% and for women to 15% (20% for working women), still much lower than the estimates of current behavior provided by the popular magazine articles cited above.

EXPLANATORY MODELS

What accounts for adultery? One can think of many different explanations, none of which exclude one another—unhappy family life, low levels of sexual activity with spouse, absence of religious and moral motivations, disorganized or troubled personal life, addictive behavior. Clearly, morality is important. The infidelity rate is only 10% for those who think that sex with someone other than a spouse is always wrong (80% of the married respondents). It rises to 70% for those who do not think it is wrong at all (1% of the married respondents). Attitudes on extramarital sex have not changed in America during the twenty years of the GSS.

The correlation of .34 between attitudes towards extramarital sex and behavior declines to .33 when frequency of church attendance and intensity of religious affiliation are taken into account, suggesting that the moral norm is independent of religious devotion.

The 1991 General Social Survey contained fifty-nine variables which could measure causes or correlates of adulterous behavior—-personal, familial, sexual, moral, psychological, religious. Since there was no theoretical reason

144

to expect any order in these variables, they were entered in a number of backward regression equations. Sexual problems with the spouse and unhappiness in the marriage disappeared early in the equations.

For men, six significant standardized predictors of infidelity emerged—in the order of importance: belief that adultery was not wrong, dissatisfaction with family life, perception of poor health, recent psychological counseling, admission of drunkenness and smoking.[4] Together these variables accounted for 28% of the variance in fidelity. Adulterous men, therefore, seem to tend to be addictive personalities with problems of mental and physical health.

The model was less effective in accounting for infidelity among women. Moral conviction, having lost a job, conflict with spouse, and trouble with a child explain 15% of the variances.[5] Unfaithful women seem driven more by relational problems than by psychological problems.

The pattern changes somewhat for (full-time) working women. Dissatisfaction with family life and psychological counseling become as important predictors for them as they are for men, accounting for .20 of the variance. Perhaps workplace pressures as well as opportunities lead to infidelity for working women. Or perhaps in the workplace women are more likely to be subject to sexual harassment or "temptation."

For men and working women there is virtually the same correlation between low levels of family satisfaction and adultery. For the nonworking women, however, there is no correlation at all. Despite the fact that working does not lower family satisfaction for women, family dissatisfaction leads to correlates with adultery for working women and not for nonworking women. Perhaps the workplace does provide alternative partners for such women. (There is no significant difference between working women and nonworking women in their disapproval of extramarital sex, and both differ significantly from married men.)

QUESTIONS

Two questions remain to be answered:

1. Why is there an impression that infidelity rates are much higher than those here reported?

2. Why are infidelity rates so low if there were evolutionary payoffs in adultery that are strong for men and, according to Fisher, also for women?

The answer to the first question might be that the rates from the Kinsey reports are so firmly fixed in our minds that they enjoy a degree of certitude not justified by the sampling process on which they were based. It also may be that certain elite classes—those who do research and those who report it in the mass media—are more prone to or have greater freedom and more opportunity for infidelity.

Even a speculative answer to the second question is more difficult to articulate. It may be that in modern western society, the structure of the lives of most men and women inhibits adultery. The sheer logistics of carrying on a love affair may preclude its possibility for many people. Moreover, it also may be that there are evolutionary mechanisms (perhaps with suitable brain chemistry) which have not been observed in other primates that facilitate the renewal of the bond. To combine these two speculations: if there is a propensity to fall in love again and again, it may simply be easier to do so with one's spouse to whom one is already "attached."

Examining such speculations in the light of data, however, must wait until research is able to focus on the "life history" of the intricate relationships, sexual and not, between man and woman, husband and wife, from the time of the beginning of love until the end of the union, either through death or divorce.

CONCLUSION

Marital infidelity is not commonplace in American society, not nearly so frequent as popular magazines and pseudoscholarship would persuade us. Nearly six out of seven married Americans have been faithful to their spouse(s). Men are more likely to be unfaithful than women, though that may be the result of fewer opportunities for women, since there is no difference between working women and men who have never engaged in "Paid Sex." The strongest predictor of fidelity is the moral principle against it which has not changed in the twenty years of the General Social Survey and which is independent of religious devotion (only 9% of those with no religious affiliation think that adultery is never wrong). There may have been an increase in infidelity in recent years because of the greater presence of women in the work force, and that may lead to a moderate increase in life-long adultery rates in years to come. An explanatory model for adultery in men invokes variables that account for one quarter of the variance and suggests emotional strains and problems in the personality of the adulterer. A model which accounts for 15% of the variance among women points more at relationship problems. However, the model for working women (explaining a fifth of the variance) is more like that of men than that of women, although there is no significant difference between the two groups of women in their disapproval of extramarital sex or their satisfaction with their family life.

In Fisher's terms the (serially) monogamous bond, perhaps "soft-wired" by evolution, is far more powerful in this country than is the propensity, also perhaps soft-wired, to adultery. The bond is very powerful indeed; even when a marriage seems to be breaking up the majority of Americans in such situations still claim to be faithful or to have been faithful. The moral norm against adultery may be all the stronger because it does not seem dependent on religious devotion. Perhaps it is something deeply rooted in the human organism, resistible indeed but itself soft-wired by the evolutionary process. Its power and its demands in the relationships between the genders ought never to be underestimated.

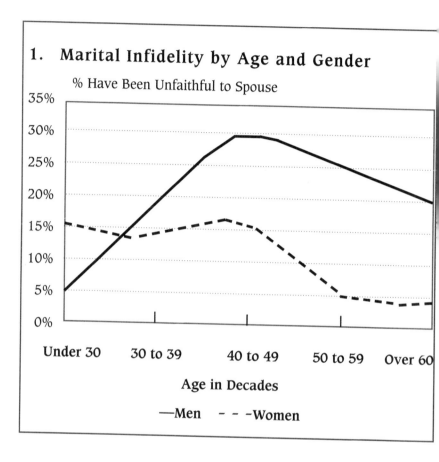

1. Marital Infidelity by Age and Gender

% Have Been Unfaithful to Spouse

Age in Decades

—Men   - - -Women

Love After Sixty

What happens to human passion as men and women grow older? It is a commonplace that it diminishes as the body weakens and the demands of the hormone system become less vigorous. Older people simply don't have sex much, or if they do, it really isn't passionate.

Or is it just possible that "senior" passion is the sweetest love available to humankind? Can it be that passionate older lovers have discovered secrets of love that younger men and women do not imagine possible?

This is a question worth addressing in this book because it would appear that the Catholic margin in frequency of sex increases in the years after 55.

My research (based as usual in this book on two national probability samples, the larger of which has more than 4400 respondents) reveals that men and women over sixty who have sex at least once a week are the most likely of any Americans to report that their marriages are very happy, that they personally are very happy, and that their life is exciting. In fact, for the latter two measures, the proportions increase with age among those who have frequent sex and decrease with age for those who don't.

Moreover, perhaps most striking of all, older men and women are the most likely of all to say that their spouse is physically attractive.

Is the spouse really that attractive? Is frequent sex most likely to continue among older people who are in fact physically attractive, or does the bemused spouse merely think that the lover is attractive? All one has to do is to ask those questions to realize how silly they are. What matters is that the spouse is attractive to the lover.

The image of passionate love between older people as grotesque is dominant in American society. Novels and films which portray such love at all, much less portray it as sensitive and appealing love, are almost nonexistent. The last great American taboo is passion among the elderly—although many of the elderly, once they know they will not be ridiculed, will testify that their sexual lives have never been more pleasurable.

As an outsider to the game of genital love, I have wondered often why sex between older lovers should be considered a subject matter for snickers and snide giggles. The longer I am around the world, the more I become aware that women do not lose their erotic appeal simply because they grow older—there are more physically attractive women in my world than there were forty years ago or even twenty years ago. Do not women react in a similar fashion to men? Might not sex become even more appealing as one has tasted more of the experiences of life and faces with a mix of acceptance and fear the inevitability of death? Might not older lovers bring more to their sexual encounters, more understanding of one another and more comprehension of what life and love mean?

It is not clear when one becomes elderly. For teenagers anyone over forty is "real old." Sex between the parents of teenagers is considered "gross" and acutely embarrassing when it produces a pregnant mother of the teen.

However, it is at least possible that it is the reaction of the "youthful" which is foolish. Might it not be that married lovers who have been together for many years have developed skills and attitudes, sensitivities and responses, respect and love, which makes sex, and especially frequent sex, more rewarding than it was when they were younger rather than less rewarding? Might the empty nest be for some people also a love nest?

My data suggests that the older lovers are the ones who are not foolish. Consider some of the findings: About one fifth of married men and women in their twenties engage in sexual intercourse less frequently than once a week. On the other hand, a more than a third of those over sixty report intercourse at least once a week and a sixth several times a week. Thus age as sheer chronology does not fate any given person to a low level of sexual activity.

Can the cherished body of the beloved still hold mystery, wonder, and surprise even after many years of marriage and the wear and tear of age? Can the impact of one's own body on the body of the beloved still be marvelous even though it has become familiar? Can the bodies of lovers still be a torment and a delight to one another after three or four decades in the same bed? If sex is (as Paul Ricoeur, the French philosopher, says) the language of tenderness, need this language ever end as long as health survives?

The sarcastic cynicism of the conventional wisdom laughs at such questions. But the data in my study suggest that for some men and women the wonderful and the marvelous has not disappeared either from the spouse's body or from one's own body.

There is certainly no inclination among the men and women over sixty to underestimate the importance of sex for holding a marriage together. In fact, they are more likely than younger men and women to say that it is a very important marriage bond. It is simply not true that after a certain age in life the importance of the sexual bond diminishes.

Some of the older men and women are very active indeed. Sixteen percent of those over sixty and 10% of those over seventy report sex MORE than once a week. Nor does their sexual activity seem to be limited to dark, awkward, and embarrassed groping late at night. Forty percent of those in their sixties and 20% of those in their seventies say that they enjoy undressing for their spouse. Twenty-seven percent and 21% respectively say that together with the spouse they engage in mutual undressing often or sometimes. A fifth of the former and a tenth of the latter report making love outdoors. Half the former and a fifth of the latter report prolonged sexual play. Sixteen percent and 12% report a shower or a bath together. Thirty-eight percent of those in their sixties and 12% of those in their seventies say that they experience ecstasy during lovemaking.

What results from an encounter between a man and a woman for whom the ambiance of their relationship is more likely to be structured by such attitudes?

Their passion is joyous in bed, but not just in the bed, nor even in the bedroom. Senior lovers each enjoy the nakedness of their own and each other's bodies as much as if not more than do other lovers. A quarter of the seniors who engage in frequent sex report that they undress each other often, more than half say that their spouse delights in them, a third say they swim together in the nude often or sometimes. A third report they shower together often or sometimes, half report extended periods of sexual play, and almost two-thirds report frequent sexual experimentation. Half say that they are not ashamed of their own nudity in the presence of their spouse and enjoy undressing their spouse.

There is a lot of very intense and very delightful sexual play taking place in the bedrooms of some senior lovers, much more of it in fact than among many younger men and women, and much reveling in the body of self and other. Approximately one out of six of all married men and women over sixty engage in frequent sex and report such reveling in undressing and being undressed. They are a minority of their age group, and they prove nothing about what others should be doing or can be doing. They merely prove that for some people the joy not only does not go out of sexual love but actually increases.

Very few people outside of those bedrooms have any idea that this is true. Even the senior lovers themselves probably think they are more exceptional than they really are.

Is sex between "senior" lovers really better than it was when they were twenty? Is it really better than the lovemaking of a married son or a daughter (who would probably be profoundly shocked if she/he knew what parents were doing)? Such questions obviously cannot be answered. What matters is that the "senior" lover is more likely to think it is better.

The senior who is a frequent lover is also notably less likely to be disappointed with both self and spouse after the sexual encounter and is likely to feel that both self and the spouse are skilled in the arts of love, while such confidence and admiration notably diminish for those who do not make love so often. Frequent successful sex with a skilled and responsive lover who is physically attractive, unashamed of nakedness, and adores you and your skill, sex which produces deep joy and is free of disappointment: is this not the *Playboy* dream come true for both husband and wife? Who could ask for anything more in the marriage bed?

This image of intense, innovative, and playful sex among those seniors who have sex at least once a week is so at odds with the cultural stereotype as to be amazing, especially since respondents over sixty are admitting to behaviors which they normally keep pretty much to themselves. If frequent sex is so sweet to those over sixty, the reason may be that they are the ones who have developed patterns of romantic playfulness earlier in life. Sexual activity diminishes with age, one might speculate, for those without such patterns and persists despite age among those who possess such patterns.

The human evolutionary process selected forms of sexual mechanics and dynamics which bonded together the male and the female in an often passionate and sometimes intensely passionate relationship so that they would preside together (in some way) over the rearing of their offspring. The evolutionary process did not need to take into account the possibility that large numbers of humans would live long after their help was no longer needed to protect neonates, infants, and children and after the fertility of the female of the species ended. Therefore, sexual attraction and frequent sexual activity in the already bonded relationship can continue (and does for 37% of the men and women in our study) long after the need of it to sustain the species has ended.

The issue of sex among the elderly (wherever one chooses to draw the line between the "young" and the "old") is a relatively new one in the human condition. For most of human history, only a few men and women managed to live to be forty-five years old, much less sixty. Those that did live to "advanced" years had probably lost their spouse and were in no position to remarry. And even if both spouses had survived, their physical health was likely to have deteriorated so that there was little opportunity for passion in their lives. It is only in this century that large numbers of men and women have survived into the "senior" category in good health and with sexual desire still very much alive, if perhaps reduced in intensity. But this change in the demography of the human condition does not seem to be matched by a change in cultural attitudes. Passionate love among the "elderly" is still viewed as grotesque and even repulsive.

Can one present in story (whether verbal or pictorial) the explicit sexual passion of older people in such a way that its full tenderness and sweetness are revealed? If it is the purpose of story to offer new visions of the possibility of life, would such portraits of passionate love not suggest both to the young and the old that intense, playful, rewarding passion need not end? Is this not wisdom that the human species needs in its new demographic situation? Sexual love defies death (as the Irish knew when they made love in the fields around the house where a wake was taking place); whether love or death is strong remains to be seen, but as the author of the *Song of Songs* says at the end, love is at least as strong as death.

So there is no reason why sexual passion among older people cannot be described both explicitly and tastefully. But such descriptions will occur only when the snide snicker of the prevailing culture is silenced by truth. At the present time, regrettably, the snicker prevails over the truth.

One suspects that the older lovers for whom passion and play have not stopped after a long life together of cherishing one another will have the last laugh. They are entitled to that laugh and they can afford to have it.

Conclusion

Catholics have sex more often than do other Americans, they are more playful in their sexual relationships, and they seem to enjoy their sexual experiences more. All of these things are true despite the repressive stance of the leadership of the Church on marital sex. While Catholics are no more likely to think of their spouses as God-like than others and no more likely to see themselves in the falling-in-love phase of a marriage, the combination of the two produces a Catholic rate of falling in love which is twenty percentage points higher than that of comparable Protestants. The correlation between a divine spouse and falling in love is six times as powerful for Catholics as it is for Protestants when one considers the amount of variance explained by the imagery of the spouse as being like God. Moreover the CHARM measures (as well as the two spouses praying together) has a stronger impact on Catholic imagery of the spouse as God-like than it does for others. In the married lives of young Catholics, religion and sex interact in subtle ways: the highest level of sexual satisfaction is to be found among those young marrieds both of whom pray often and have warm religious imagery. Despite the sexual abuse problem, confidant relationships between a married woman and a priest tend on the average to lead to a happier marriage for her and her husband and more sexual satisfaction for the husband. Older Catholics are especially more likely to engage in both frequent intercourse and sexual play than their counterparts who are not Catholic. All of these unique dimensions of Catholic sexuality can be attributed to the popular tradition of the Catholic heritage and to the imagery in that tradition of a spousal image of God.

If, as I have contended, we organize our lives around stories by which we explain to ourselves and to others what our lives mean, a crucial part of the story of our life is the story of our intimate relationships and particularly a relationship with a spouse. Catholicism, precisely because it sees human relationships as metaphors (analogies) for the relationship between God and humans, provides a powerful repertory of such stories for those who are part of its tradition, especially the story of a bond between man and woman that is comparable in power to the bond between God and Her people.

Catholic canon law and certain kinds of Catholic theology defend strongly the notion of the marriage bond. However, they seem to mean a contractual bond that is established by the consent of the partners and cannot after a certain state of development (intercourse and, according to more recent theories, emotional maturity) be sundered by any power but death.

While such an approach might have its merits, it seems to underestimate the physical and biological power of the bond described in Chapter Nine. It is clear to the evolutionary biologists that all the complexity and variety, all the intensity and the pleasure, all the frustrations and the joys of human sexual union are ordered towards bonding the man and the woman together so they will be able to see their offspring into adulthood. The progress of the human species into its present condition required that its neonates be protected and trained by their parents for a long period of time. Unlike other higher primates, humans do not abandon their young as soon as they are able to feed themselves. Indeed, as human parents know perhaps too well, the task only begins when the kid has learned to put food into its mouth with reasonable civility.

All that is unique to human sexuality in comparison with the other higher primates (especially the chimpanzees with whom we share almost 99% of genetic inheritance) is ordered in one way or another towards bonding—(relative) monogamy, the larger size of the woman compared to that of other higher primate females relative to the size of their spouse, the constant availability for sex, the frequency of sex (Gorilla females have sex only once every couple of years), the secondary sexual characteristics (alone of the primates, women's breasts develop before the birth of the first child), modesty, the privacy of lovemaking, the secrecy of ovulation, menopause, sex after fertility has ended. None of these uniquely human sexual characteristics are required for reproduction. All were selected by the evolutionary process to contribute to bonding. The bonds can be broken and sometimes are because humans are not prisoners of the genetic inheritance which evolution has imposed on them. But the bonds are nonetheless powerful and far more than just an irrevocably binding legal contract. As scientist Jared Diamond puts it, "In no species besides humans has the purpose of copulation become so unrelated to reproduction."

It must be emphasized that Professor Diamond is not speaking from a deductive and a prioristic perspective. He is simply describing what we know about higher primates, indeed about all animals.

Some Catholics object to this comparison with animals. Humans are not just apes and must govern their behavior by higher standards than those for which evolution has selected. We should not be obsessed with sexual pleasure the way animals are. In fact, however, such an argument is unfair to animals who are not nearly as obsessed with sexuality as we are. In other species of higher primates, reproduction is relatively simple compared to that in humans—a brief interlude of copulation when the female is in "estrus." Primate sexuality is in general restrained, especially when compared with our sexuality. In no species are the bonding aspects of sex so elaborate or so powerful and in no species are animals so preoccupied by sex as humans are. Again, as Professor Diamond puts it, "In no species besides humans has the purpose of copulation become so unrelated to reproduction." Diamond is not describing a theoretical or deductive theory of human nature. Rather he is describing the nature of human nature as it appears in the comparative study of animals (of which we are, by the way, one). The evolutionary process selected a complex, intricate, demanding, and powerfully pleasurable sexual relationship for humans because it was so absolutely essential to bond the parents of human offspring together.

Indeed, it is the somewhat narrow official Catholic view of sexual intercourse that equates us with animals: Human intercourse is for reproduction. All else is secondary. The "unhonest" ("inhonestum" of sexual love, "dirty" if one wishes) aspects of human copulation can be tolerated because without them humans would not copulate and there would be no offspring. But in the absence of a some link to reproduction, this "unhonest" dimension becomes morally wrong. Humans are not supposed to enjoy the pleasures of sex unless in some fashion reproduction is possible.[1] To argue this position means to ignore completely the bonding powers of sexual pleasure. Indeed it demeans the bonding power and even in effect forbids it.

As I have argued previously, the Church has undervalued (for reasons which need not detain us) the bonding component of human sexual pleasure. I doubt that there is a serious evolutionary biologist or comparative primatologist in the world who would question Professor Diamond's description of the nature of human nature as sexual. Nor do I think many married laity or parish clergy would question it either.

But Church leaders dismiss it, to the extent that they even know about it—and it is my impression that very few have ever heard of evolutionary biology. The study of natural law has come a long way from Thomas Aquinas for whom it was an empirical study.[2] Whatever the human sciences may say about the nature of human nature is either wrong or not to be considered if it seems to be in disagreement with what Church leaders KNOW to be true.

It is hard for me to see how this implicit rejection (often through culpable ignorance) of the human sciences on the nature of human sexuality (which by the way imply strong arguments for monogamy and family) is any different from the rejection of Galileo on the motion of the stars and the planets. Everything had to revolve around the earth because Church leaders said it was that way. Human sexuality is not primarily for bonding the spouses together because Church leaders say that it is not. Humans may not engage in sex merely for bonding (even though that seems to them and to the human scientists the most natural thing to do) because Church leaders say they can't.

It is a position with which one cannot argue. Nor is it up to me to argue. I must be content with repeating what the human sciences (and the married laity) say about human sexuality and ask whether the Church ought not to try to integrate this wisdom into its teaching.

The Church's own metaphors suggest that the sexual bond is a story of human love, triumphant, defeated, and resurgent. The bonding love between God and humans is not the story of a single act or a group of single acts but rather a story of long and frequently reinforced relationship, one that is (from the human viewpoint at any rate) often marked by diminution and resurgence, decline and growth, near-death and rebirth, pleasure and pain and yet more pleasure. It is precisely this kind of imagery which has made the Catholic experience of sex as described in this book somewhat unique; and it is this imagery to which Catholics turn when they must make decisions about sex.

The stories contained in the profoundly Catholic images of "Spouse," "Lover," "Mother," and "Friend" are all stories of pleasure and passion that are sustained through a long process of bonding and not merely in certain isolated acts. Poets who explore these metaphors would have no trouble accepting the evolutionary biologists' conclusions about the nature of human nature and of human sexual love. Indeed, poets would probably marvel at how wondrous the combination of events in the evolutionary process were to have produced such a powerful bonding force, with its agonies and ecstasies that are unique to humankind.

FOOTNOTES

Introduction

1. Many of the projects going on in various countries seem almost fixated on condom use as safe sex against AIDS and thus ignore the evidence in their own tables that far more people are protected from AIDS by monogamy than by condoms.
2. I develop and test this premise at great length in my book *Religion as Poetry* (Translation Publishers, Fall 1994.) The religious story is a model which humans impose on the cosmos to make sense and purpose out of their lives. Most scientists and most social scientists would probably contend that the models are nothing more than constructs which, while they may be necessary for humans, do not correspond to any reality (not to say Reality) which actually can be found in a senseless and purposeless cosmos. However, such a determination goes beyond the boundaries of science and becomes a matter of faith. One could just as well commit oneself in an equal leap of faith to the conviction that religious stories resonate in deep metaphor to processes at work in the cosmos itself. Some scientists now insist that the cosmos itself is a story or at least has a story. Brian Swimme, in "The Cosmic Creation Story" (*The Reenchantment of Science*, ed. David Ray Griffin, State UNY Press, 1989) contends that at the most basic level the universe is not so much matter or energy or information but story. While it does not follow that the universe story correlates with religious story, but correlation is at least a possibility.

Chapter One

1. As Catholic bishops call themselves, apparently unaware that they have taken over a nineteenth-century Lutheran term.
2. A riposte to this might be phrased in the words of a woman on Irish radio, "Sure, aren't Irish men closet lovers?"

Chapter Two

1. In my early days in the confessional in the late 1950s, birth control was still occasionally confessed as "race suicide."
2. Both Catholic School studies were based on representative probability samples of American Catholics. The margin of error at the .01 level would not exceed three percentage points in either direction.
3. Samuel H. Preston. "Family Sizes of Children and Family Sizes of Women," Demography 13: 105-114. Feb. 1976. Preston's correction factor enables one to estimate the average size of a parental generation from the average number of siblings in the family of respondents. I assume a quarter century between generations.

4. In *From Now to Zero: Fertility and Contraception and Abortion in America*. Boston: Little Brown, 1968.

5. I find myself wondering whether one of the reasons that Pope Paul VI thought he could reverse the trends by his birth control encyclical *Humanae Vitae* was that he remembered the early successes of the campaign after *Casti Connubii*. Did he think that he could repeat the process by activating the loyalty of bishops and priests and constraining the lay people to do what he thought they should do? If he did, he surely missed the signs of the times. The clergy had troubled the consciences of the laity, and the laity, especially in the English-speaking world, permitted their consciences to be troubled—up to a point. Both groups had made up their minds that it didn't work and were not about to give it another try. This judgment is not an ethical one on my part but a simple description of what happened.

6. Question wording: "A married couple who feel they have as many children as they want are really not doing anything wrong when they use an artificial means to prevent conception."

7. Question wording: "Do you think the Catholic Church has the right to teach what positions Catholics should take on . . . proper means for family limitation?"

8. Question wordings:
"Husband and wife may have sexual intercourse for pleasure alone."
"A family should have as many children as possible and God will provide for them."

Chapter Three

1. A random sample of 1308 American married men and women interviewed in a telephone survey by the Gallup organization. The details of the research are reported in *Faithful Attraction*.

2. In the questionnaire god begins with a small "g," I suspect because the devout Catholic study director at Gallup was uneasy about apparent blasphemy. However, those interviewed on the phone did not know about the small "g." I will spell God with an uppercase "G" and refer to the spouse using the phrases "as God-Like" or "as a God" interchangeably.

3. See *Faithful Attraction*.

4. Ibid.

5 No one has guessed either the most powerful factor or the three most powerful factors yet.

6. "Mysterious" has the strongest correlation of the four variables with a God-like spouse when the factor is disassembled. The other three variables have equal impact. The God-like spouse then is an exciting, romantic, well-dressed mystery, one you

enjoy disrobing for and enjoy undressing and in whose presence you feel little embarrassment about your naked body or about sexual love.

7. There are some differences in the models for men and women, for the young, and the old, and for Catholics and Protestants. Charm and nakedness are equally important for men and for women, however, and more important for the older than for the younger and much more important for Catholics than for Protestants.

8. Or him. But the CHARM variable has, as we have seen, more impact on a man's seeing his woman as God-like than vice versa. It may well be that in our culture women are indeed more "adorable." Or maybe in any culture. Since being mysterious, exciting, and romantic (and perhaps even a sharp dresser) are good things to be, this fact could be seen as discrimination against women only if they were placed under undue constraints to develop these admirable characteristics. It might be a better world if men were more powerfully motivated to develop such traits.

9. "Sharp Dresser" is probably a surrogate for "elegant" or "tasteful."

10. Pp 106 to 112 of *Original Unity of Man and Woman*. Boston: Daughters of Saint Paul, 1981. This translation of the audience talks is taken from the Vatican newspaper, *Osservatore Romano*.

11. In his audience talks on human sexuality, Pope John Paul II suggested just such an experience but at a level of abstraction so high that no one seems to have noticed the suggestion.

Chapter Four

1. Married scholars cooperated with me at every step of the research process.

2. P 667, *The Marital Sacrament*. Mahwah NJ: Paulist Press, 1989.

3. Ibid.

4. Op.cit., page 669.

5. Question wording: "Many people think that marriages go through cycles—over and over again. If the cycles are falling in love, settling down, bottoming out, and beginning again, where would you put your marriage at the present time?"

6. "Would you say your spouse is sometimes like a God to you?"

7. There are, in general, no statistically significant gender correlations in the findings reported in the last several paragraphs. However, it is true that erotic play is more important for women over forty years old than it is either for younger women or for men—and because such play enhances their self-image.

Chapter Five

1. *The Young Catholic Family: Religious Images and Marriage Fulfillment,* Andrew M. Greeley. Chicago: Thomas More, 1980.

2. The Young Catholic project did not analyze young people going through the years of their marriage, a process which would have required repeated returns to the same respondents (and for which the Knights, unhappy with our findings and with me for my novel writing, were not about to fund). Thus I am forced to assume that the snapshot of different times of marriage duration available to us is also a hint of a life cycle experience.

3. In analysis subsequent to the research reported in this chapter, Michael Hout and I demonstrated that the phenomenon reported here could be generalized. There is a stable life-cycle curve of religious behavior which has remained largely invariant among American Catholics since 1975.

Chapter Six

1. I note, as I always do when studying such matters, that only a fool would argue that the Church should change its doctrine to keep up with the times. One does not arrive at moral judgments by counting noses. Nor does one derive ethical systems from surveys. Moral theology (by whatever name) tries to describe what the good life is. Sociology tries to describe how life is actually lived. There can be no opposition between the two because, as we used to say, they have different formal objects. Church persons should listen to sociology not because it will provide them with moral judgments but because it will tell them the nature of the environment in which they must work and perhaps because it will provide them with some material for theological reflection.

   In addition to this standard warning of my position, I must add that on the subject of single sex I have always suspected that sex without public commitment is fraught with dangers of deception, self-deception, and exploitation, particularly of women by men.

Chapter Eight

1. There was some loud criticism of an earlier version of this chapter on the grounds that I should have included in my denominator all priests active in the archdiocese, including religious order priests. However, the cardinal's commission reviewed only archdiocesan priests. So the denominator is correct and the 3.27% rate is correct. (If one included all archdiocesan priests who were active in the archdiocese during the quarter century covered in the commissions review, the rate would have been closer to 5%.)

Chapter Nine

1. *Anatomy of Love: The Natural History of Monogamy, Adultery, and Divorce*, Helen E. Fisher, Norton: New York, 1992.
2. Fisher speculates that "infatuation" is caused in part by an "excitant amine" called phenylethylamine or PEA and "attachment" (a subsequent and more peaceful if not so exciting relationship) by the endorphins "calming" the fervor of "falling in love."
3. The wording of the question implies that it pertains to all marriages and not just the present marriage
4. Question wordings:
   —"What is your opinion about a married person having sexual relations with someone other than the marriage partner— is it always wrong, almost always wrong, only sometimes wrong, or not wrong at all."
   —" . . . how much satisfaction do you get from family life—a very great deal, a great deal, quite a bit, a fair amount, some, a little, none."
   —"Would you say your own health, in general is excellent, good, fair or poor?"
   —In the last twelve months did "any of the following happen to you. . . . Underwent counseling for mental or emotional problems?"
   —"Do you sometimes drink more than you think you should?"
   —"Do you smoke?"
5. Question wording:
   —"During the last year were you fired or permanently laid off?"
   —"During the past year did you have serious trouble with your husband?"
   —"During the past year did your child have serious trouble in school (e.g. failing, dropping out, expelled, held back)?"

Conclusion

1. How anything which God put into the world to bond men and women together in love can be considered dirty escapes me. More to the point for the history of Catholic sexual ethics, however, St. Augustine had no problem deciding that it was in fact dirty.
2. In the *Summa Contra Gentiles* Thomas Aquinas argues that one learns third-level principles of the natural law from a study of what is done in the nations—in the *gentes* to use his word.